Why I Stay

Why I Stay

The Challenges of Discipleship
for Contemporary Mormons

ROBERT A. REES, EDITOR

Signature Books • Salt Lake City • 2011

Design by Connie Disney

Cover by Ron Stucki

Why I Stay was printed on acid-free paper and was composed, printed, and bound in the United States of America.

15   14   13   12   11   5   4   3   2   1

www.signaturebooks.com

Library of Congress Cataloging-in-Publication Data
Why I stay : the challenges of discipleship for contemporary
Mormons / edited by Robert A. Rees.
    p. cm.
  Includes bibliographical references.
  ISBN 1-56085-213-5 (978-1-56085-213-1 : alk. paper)
1. Mormons—Religious life. 2. Church of Jesus Christ of
Latter-day Saints—Membership. I. Rees, Robert A., 1935-
editor.
  BX8656.W55 2011
  248.4'893—dc23   2011030893

Contents

Editor's Introduction

> "Lord, to whom shall we go?
> Thou hast the words of eternal life."
> —Peter to Jesus (John 6:68)

Deciding whether to stay in or leave one's faith tradition is among the most difficult and soul-wrenching decisions a person can face. There are those who feel firmly rooted in their religion for a lifetime; others bolt from a church, temple, or mosque suddenly, impulsively, and ultimately; still others lapse, as Emily Dickinson said of the passing of summer, "as imperceptibly as grief." There are believers who experience the tension between the impulse to leave and the magnetic pull to stay. Those who experience little or no tension see staying as axiomatic and sail forever on a calm sea of devotion. Others who experience periodic or even constant tension navigate their way on a turbulent sea of faith and reason, of belief and doubt, of individual conscience and institutional devotion. Over the course of a lifetime, a few Saints ebb and flow between the poles of going and staying.

All religions have a problem with retention. Even Jesus had difficulty retaining his disciples, judging from the fast falling away of some followers while he was still alive: "From this time many of his disciples turned back and no longer followed him" (John 6:66, New International Version). This is foreshadowed in Jesus's Parable of the Sower where it seems that more of his seeds (followers) fell by the wayside, fell on stony ground, and fell among thorns than the few that fell on good earth. Even among the latter, fewer still remained fully faithful by yielding "a hundredfold" (Matt. 13:1-23).

There are many reasons why people stay in a religion and many reasons why they leave. Not all reasons for staying are motivated by faith and loyalty nor all those for leaving motivated by faithlessness and disloyalty. That is, some are kept in the fold by fear and some leave out of self-preservation. Some stay because they find holiness in the Restored Gospel; others leave because they find a more holy and hospitable place elsewhere. Many who leave their Church gravitate to other Churches. In an article titled "Faith in Flux," Patricia Zapor, citing a study by the Pew Forum on Religion & Public Life, states, "When the number of people who now practice a different faith than that of their childhood is added to those who have moved around among religions or denominations and come back to where they started, nearly half of Americans have changed religions at some point."

It is interesting to note that many of those who leave the LDS Church (either officially or unofficially) stay emotionally connected to Mormon culture, if not to the Church itself. This is attested by the number of ex-Mormon groups that attempt both to justify their leaving and to persuade others to follow them, including the following:

- Exmormon Foundation
- Ex-Mormons for Jesus
- Mormon No More
- PostMormon Community
- Recovery from Mormonism

There are also those who leave the Church spiritually but not physically, those who leave it physically but not spiritually, and those who try for some accommodation between the two. New Order Mormons (NOM), for instance, encourages members to stay in spite of disagreement over certain teachings and practices.

For those who remain in the Church, there is an inevitable sadness over those who leave. This sadness is compounded when the reasons for leaving are un-Christianlike treatment by Church leaders or members or when the rupture in the relationship was preventable by greater compassion and charity. Part of the sadness is because separation from the body of saints often means a sacrifice of shared intimacy and joy and the conviction that some eternal bond has been frayed or broken, with both mortal and eternal consequences. I suspect that each contributor to this volume has family and friends who no longer consider themselves members of the fold and therefore the authors' staying is motivated in part by the hope that their faithfulness might ultimately be persuasive to others.

What seems evident from the personal expressions of faith, challenge, and devotion in this collection is that many contemporary Latter-day Saints remain committed to the Church in spite of personal difference or spiritual dissonance over beliefs, doctrines, and practices. For some, like Lael Littke, leaving has been a temptation they have felt on occasion but have successfully resisted; for others, leaving has never been a considered option. As Armand Mauss writes, "I have never contemplated leaving." Mary Bradford echoes this sentiment when she says, "My first thought is where I might go if I weren't [Mormon]. The Church is my village and my home." Although his essay includes reasons why he stays "in spite of" difficulties, Bill Bradshaw says that he remains because he wants to, that he has not had a serious inclination to leave. This epitomizes the view of most thoughtful, faithful Mormons, including those who contributed essays to this collection. Cherry Silver expresses similar sentiments: "I stay in the Church because this is the only way of life that seems real to me." Her sister-in-law, Claudia Bushman, agrees, saying, "My question is not why I stay in the Church, but why should I leave?" She adds, "I love the Church. I don't want to leave it. My Church experience and identity are deeply ingrained. It may even come before my identity as a woman. It certainly comes before my identity as an American."

Greg Prince takes a pragmatic view: "On a variety of levels, the Church learns from its mistakes and continues forward while I do the same. It has its share of problems, as do other Churches, and as we work to resolve, rather than ignore, those problems, we and the Church become better." Fred Christensen accepts the Church's problems as a necessary part of enjoying its blessings: "I believe the Church has been a contributing factor to my good life. I am disturbed by much of the Church's orthodoxy, but I have managed to discount it in the balance. I think there is room in the Church for differing views. At least, I hope others who have views like mine are consoled that I remain, while those whose views are different will continue to tolerate me." Charlotte England acknowledges that the road was not always smooth in the Church for her and her husband, Gene, but that leaving would have meant "abandoning our core beliefs, which were too deeply embedded for us to forsake."

A number of contributors feel a strong connection to their pioneer heritage and a religious commitment to their own families. Some are fifth- and sixth-generation Latter-day Saints and feel, as Toby Pingree, that they are "Mormon to [their] bones." "I stay because of my heritage," writes Bill Bradshaw, "because of those who came before me to whom I am indebted, because of sacrifices of which I am only dimly aware but which have made life and faith possible." Some feel a similar hold not only because of an obligation to past generations but also because of a stewardship to current and future generations. Tom Rogers says, "I am locked in by extensive ancestral and familial ties. As a father of seven and grandfather of thirty-seven, I sufficiently appreciate the Church's blessing to my progeny that I do not want to discourage their attachment to it. I realize that, by itself, this is a strictly pragmatic, subjective, and ultimately inadequate criterion, but I offer it here for the sake of candor."

Some believers maintain their faith, to use the title of Morris Thurston's essay, by "Taking the Long View." Like Thurston, they feel they can make a difference. As he states, "I stay, hoping that my voice and others can help prompt changes for the good, but all the while understanding my own limitations. I know that, like all fallible and imperfect humans, I could be mistaken. However, I also know that it is my Christian responsibility to speak as honestly as I can and as humbly as I am able. I stay because I believe that doing so can make a difference." Molly Bennion, taking advice from an early conversation with Lowell Bennion, states simply, "I stay to serve and bless and to be served and be blessed," a sentiment that is in one way or another echoed by all of the contributors.

The essays included here were all presented between August 2003 and August 2010 at the Why I Stay session of the annual Sunstone Symposium in Salt Lake City. Originated and organized by Toby Pingree, whose own essay is included here, this annual session remains one of the most inspirational and popular for Sunstone attendees. The reason will be immediately apparent to readers.

The authors represent people from a wide range of professions—physicians, attorneys, university professors and administrators, entrepreneurs, and independent scholars, as well as poets, playwrights, novelists, historians, and biographers. In terms of Church service, they include ward and stake Relief Society, Primary, and Young Women's presidents and General Board Members as well as bishops, stake presidents, mission presidents, temple presidents, and patriarchs. Mostly, they have a mature faith, one, to use Chase Peterson's words, that is expressed "with neither smothering insistence nor smug aloofness, with neither blind faith nor blind rejection, with intense individuality, anchored in free agency and a growing appreciation for [a] historic and current debt to many good Church leaders and ... fellow Saints."

In my opinion, one of the most exemplary examples of devotion among contemporary Latter-day Saints is that of one of the contributors, Lavina Fielding Anderson, who is technically no longer a member of the Church. As an excommunicated Mormon, she is, to use her words, "*of* but not *in* the Church." I do not know of another Mormon in the entire sweep of Church history who has remained as faithful in her commitment to Mormonism in the face of a two-decade-long excommunication, especially for what many feel were insufficient grounds for so draconian a punishment. "Week after week, month after month, year after year," Lavina has continued to attend her local ward and perform the most menial of tasks, which are the only ones permitted by her status. She lists six reasons why she stays, the most important of which is that she sees "the world Mormonly. ... [Mormonism constitutes] my people, my music, my mode of prayer, my history, my family."

I was touched recently in reading Jan Shipps's account of her own response to Lavina's excommunication the Sunday following the event. It happened to be "worldwide communion Sunday, the day on which Christians all over the world—no matter how divided in other ways—become one, ritually re-constituting the body of Christ in space and time." As a lay participant in the Eucharistic ritual in her own Church, Jan, recognizing that her friend and sister Lavina was unable to take the sacrament in her own Church and following the Mormon concept of proxy ordinances, took the sacrament "for and in behalf" of Lavina. As Jan writes, "When death— or excommunication, which is a kind of death—makes it impossible for people to participate in needed ritual acts, the Saints know that a brother or sister in Christ can perform that act for them. Knowing that, I remembered my taking of the bread and wine and understood the concept of participation in rituals by proxy. It comforted me. And I am certain that Lavina was comforted, too."

The only other non-Latter-day Saint, but nevertheless Mormon, included in this collection is Bill Russell, a member of the Community of Christ Church and long-time friend of Latter-day Saints. Russell, like some of his Latter-day Saint counterparts in this anthology, has wrestled with such issues as racism, sexism, homophobia, and political conservatism within his own faith tradition and yet has chosen to remain actively engaged in the Community of Christ, working for change. He says, "If the Church had not changed its direction, I would not be actively involved in it today. I stayed to become more active today than ever before."

Russell's experience parallels that of many other contributors who have found themselves at odds with the Church over such issues as polygamy, the ordination of blacks to the priesthood, women's rights, the treatment of homosexuals (including, more recently, same-sex marriage), and independent thinking and expression. As Toby Pingree says, such issues "have been and continue to be troublesome to my faith." While others have found such issues sufficient reason to separate themselves from the Church, many Latter-day Saints, including the writers of these essays, have found a way to hold on to their faith in spite of their differences with the Church and because they also find meaning, nurturance, and joy as members. As Claudia Bushman puts it, "Why

would I even think of leaving the Church? I'm happy here."
This sounds ironic after her acknowledgment of difficulties,
but she is nevertheless serious. She is quick to add this adden-
dum: "I certainly hope and pray that the Church does not
decide to leave me."

Contemporary Latter-day Saints such as those represent-
ed in this anthology have made what theologian Paul Tillich
called an "ultimate commitment." In his essay, Tom Rogers
explains that "in all religions, the principle of obedience to
God is fundamental. If we are potentially glorious, as the Restored Gospel tells us we are, it is also true that we are infinitesimal in the scheme of our Creator's grand universe. This
paradox requires that, should we sufficiently believe it, we no
longer have a choice about our future" and need to submit
fully to whatever God intends for us.

Many contributors have played roles in building up the
Church away from the central stakes of the Mormon Corridor, finding dynamic opportunities to expand their faith in
other regions of the United States and on other continents.
As one Latter-day Saint serving a mission in Eastern Europe
expressed it, "When you're working in a primary way with the
basic principles of the gospel and with people who are learning them for the first time, there is little room or luxury for
criticism or negativity." There is also room to find one's way
without the expectations imposed on people in the Mormon
Corridor. Grethe Peterson writes:

> Many of my spiritual guides and teachers have been
> outside our Church. ... The wisdom and goodness of
> these women deeply touched my soul, changing me for-
> ever. Much of my growth has been the result of turn-
> ing inward, of getting to know my soul and heart con-
> nections, separating ego from true belief. To know that
> God the Eternal Father, our Mother in Heaven, and our

brother Jesus Christ are my mentors, and my strength, keeps me hopeful and moving forward. My life experiences have taught me the beauty and value of diversity. We may not look or think alike, but we are all God's children. We are all equal before our Lord, so our ability to reach out to one another brings us closer to heaven.

Being involved in the conversion of other people can also further solidify one's own commitment. As a Church patriarch to "the vast territory of Eastern Europe," Tom Rogers adds, "Each time I travel abroad on this assignment, I witness the transformation in the lives of those I interview which, as they frequently testify, took place when they acquired a testimony through the Spirit's transcendent power." He says that "their determination to exercise the discipline necessary to change, often dramatically," strengthens his own belief.

Many contributors feel that they show their love and devotion to the Church when they seek to improve it, to see it more perfectly reflect the gospel of Christ. The pursuit of that ideal has sometimes elicited criticism from fellow members and drawn official and unofficial censure from Church leaders. This can leave one feeling isolated and lonely. Nevertheless, most find fellowship in their local congregations. As Armand Mauss states, "I know that outside of my immediate family, my ward community cares more about me and my wife than does any other community in the world."

In Mormonism, as in any religion, there are markers of devotion or, perhaps one might say, orthodoxy—signs and symbols, formulaic phrases, communal rituals that generally indicate a person's unquestioned involvement with and acceptance by their religious society. For example, Mormons are famous for declaring with absolute certainty, "I know," but there are some who, in spite of a lifetime of seeking, are unable to speak such words. Karen Rosenbaum says, "I have never been able to say 'This is true' about spiritual life in general or about Mormonism in particular. Despite decades of immersion in Mormonism, despite prayer and study, I feel I *know* almost nothing." Not being able to "bear testimony" in the conventional and particular Mormon way can make one feel marginalized in the Church, especially if one also expresses uncertainty about God and the very nature of things, as does Karen. Her candid insights remind me of Emily Dickinson, who felt out of place in her very Puritan (and very Mormon-like) community. She spoke of her inability to give the expected confession of faith when she was a student at Mount Holyoke College, seeing herself as "the only kangaroo among the beauty."

Most of the present contributors speak of finding something of great value in their lifetime of devotion in spite of periodic estrangement and occasional (or even persistent) discomfort. Some are held by their own faith, others by the faith of family and friends. Some stay in the hope that their continuing activity may result in their being, to use C. S. Lewis's phrase, "surprised by Joy." As Karen Rosenbaum puts it in remembering Eugene England's account of an experience he had while attending a stake conference as a twelve-year-old and feeling "the presence of the Holy Ghost," "perhaps if I stay in the Church, some day, because I am *there,* I will be touched in that way. Perhaps I will be able to brush off my warty little soul and *will* myself to leap to hope and eternal meaning."

In "My Reasons and Motivations," Jeff Burton imagines a Church in which no one would ever have cause or wish to leave, a Church in which those things that either drive or tempt people to leave simply don't exist. It is a Church like one might imagine in the city of Enoch. Burton says, in imagining himself a member of such an idealized church, "I have such a feeling of belonging and being cherished. Why wouldn't I stay?" One can find elements of that ideal Church in the personal expressions of both devotion and hope in this collection.

In his sonnet, "The Silken Tent," Robert Frost uses an extended metaphor to characterize the paradoxical tensions and ties that coexist in a loving, intimate relationship. While his poem is about a woman ("She is as in a field a silken tent"), I think it also works for any deep and complex relationship, including religious devotion. The tent is held up by a

> ... supporting central cedar pole,
> That is its pinnacle to heavenward
> And signifies the sureness of the soul ...

The heat of the sun affects the tent so that

> At midday when the sunny summer breeze
> Has dried the dew and all its ropes relent,
> [The tent] gently sways at ease ... [and]
> Seems to owe naught to any single cord,
> But strictly held by none, is loosely bound
> By countless silken ties of love and thought
> To everything on earth the compass round ...

I believe the contributors to this volume help hold up the tent of faith by a devotion characterized "by countless silken ties of love and thought" and the "supporting central pole" that signifies the sureness of their souls. Whether the Church recognizes and rewards such faithfulness, I believe it is vital to the Church's future flowering and its ultimate destiny.

It Satisfies My Restless Mind

Thomas F. Rogers

I have never seriously contemplated leaving the Church, although I have imaginatively identified with those who have, among them a few lifelong friends. I have written plays about two excommunicants, Helmuth Huebener and John D. Lee,[1] who, although they did not choose to be disenfranchised, were, at the end of their lives, equally alienated. I may at times resonate to Yeats's profound lines: "The best lack all conviction, while the worst are full of passionate intensity."[2] It is a temptation to sometimes simplistically apply such a label to fellow Saints, many of them being nevertheless devoted friends and neighbors.

I suppose I have been spared the test of faith and humility with which, in whatever form, ecclesiastical censure ensues. This may be due to my essentially deferential (perhaps cowardly and obsequious) personality. Along with my respect for the sanity and moderation advocated by a former Jordanian ambassador, Muhammad Kamal,[3] and the cardinal Christian virtues of charity and humility stressed by Reinhold Niebuhr, I strongly sense the practical need to defer, to accommodate, to fit in—for which the closest equivalent I can find in scripture is temperance.

Sometimes simply turning away from a difficult or potentially disturbing situation seems like the best response. The Utah poet Magdalene Young Hanson Warren notes the response of two of Noah's sons to their father's nakedness: they turned their heads and made nothing more of it.[4] In various ecclesiastical roles, I have benefited from others' sustaining support, which when it is withheld or not manifest diminishes one's ability to function in their behalf.

I am a product of the "know nothing, do nothing" generation that came of age after World War II. In the Church, this coincided with the ecclesiastical helmsmanship of the ever so compassionate and genteel David O. McKay. President McKay was amicably disposed to the life of the mind and was, in hindsight, legendary in his tolerance. Sterling McMurrin once recounted to me the cases of various LDS Institute of Religion teachers and others who had come under fire and for whom he intervened with President McKay. That McMurrin had such entrée with the president speaks volumes about that leader's large-souled openness. On more than one occasion, I have been the less-than-perfect recipient of such acceptance and good will from Church leaders.

In this regard, I think of the four BYU Russian professors who have served as mission presidents in the former Soviet Union. Each of my former colleagues had remarkable administrative skills, but these were less evident in Salt Lake at the time of their calls than among professional executives who are more routinely called to such positions. For instance, Gary Browning's role in the early days of the Church in Russia was truly groundbreaking and highly effective. Even so, no one was more surprised by his call than he was. He had earlier headed up the small BYU chapter of scholars opposed to the nuclear arms race and had, he felt, incurred considerable displeasure from various ultra-orthodox conservatives in Salt Lake City. There is no question that we four were seen as especially useful because of our language background and that this helped prompt the extension of such a privileged trust, but I like to think that, despite our less-than-already-proven reputations and in some cases our dubious political correctness, surprisingly fruitful outcomes resulted from that wider sharing of such a weighty stewardship.

Allow me now to suggest at least six reasons for my active engagement in Church life:

1. I am locked in by extensive ancestral and familial ties. As a father of seven and grandfather of thirty-seven, I sufficiently appreciate the Church's blessing to my progeny that I do not want to discourage their attachment to it. I realize that, by itself, this is a strictly pragmatic, subjective, and ultimately inadequate criterion, but I offer it here for the sake of candor.

2. There is nothing better out there, in my opinion. Few religions are nearly so comprehensive in addressing the individual and group needs of their adherents. A non-believing former member tells me he still considers the Church to have the "most comprehensive social benefit program" he has ever encountered. I agree. For instance, what contribution hasn't the Word of Wisdom alone made to my personal well-being? What downside has there been to my association with people with whom I disagree on many points and with whom I otherwise have very little in common? It has stretched me, made me feel less elitist—and maybe them too. Would my saintly wife have even settled for me if I had been a more selfish and self-absorbed career-minded individual, without the nudging of the Church to be more other-directed and well-rounded? Would our children be such decent, caring people? This may still not be a good enough reason to stay, but it is a factor.

3. I have a testimony of the inspiration behind the Church. A testimony is a gift—in the Mormon view, an earned one. It is a choice too, and not a bad one. As Mother Teresa said, "If

you pray, you will have faith. And if you have faith, you will love. And if you love, you will serve. And if you serve, you will have peace."[5] A great-great-grandfather's sacrifices doubly charged me and his now vast progeny. After barely surviving the march of the Mormon Battalion, Thomas Karren was called to leave his family and serve a mission to the Sandwich Islands. Hawaii wasn't a tourist mecca then, and a number of those first missionaries did not hold out. One sentence leaps at me from his missionary journal, this one dated February 17, 1854: "There is nothing but a realizing sense of the duty I owe to my Priesthood and Calling as a minister of Christ that would induce me for one moment to stop here and live in the manner I have."

4. The Restored Gospel's explanation of life and human destiny satisfies my restless and contemplative mind. It appeals to me much like Joseph Smith described certain truths as "tasting good," and many of its practical emphases strike me as truly remarkable. I briefly mention four:

- The concept of family continuity and eternal lives. Certain critics deride this concept as being non-Christian, as well as its corollary of divine heirship, but I find them existentially right and highly edifying.

- The balance between faith and reason, obedience and personal revelation. I respond with a resounding *Yes!* to the image of a faith-traveler's holding onto an iron rod while also responding to the less-tangible illumination of an individual Liahona. While studying a range of belief systems and interacting in Russia with people from many denominations, I've been made aware of how rare such balance really is. In many religious traditions, one worships, trance-like, by completely turning off one's critical faculties and hypnotically chanting, fingering beads, or repeating set prayers. At the other end of the spectrum are those who relish speculation at the expense of doctrine and structure so that anything goes. I value how, at least in theory, Mormonism tries to modify both approaches.

- The Church keeps pace with life's constant fluctuations, fully taking into account the mutual interdependence of individuals at all stages of the life cycle. In its daily operations and wide focus, the Church manages to respond not only to our constantly mutating individual lives but also—through its great attention to those of a younger age—to the inevitable displacement and succession by one generation of the next. While many other traditions focus more narrowly on the single relationship between the individual and her God or priest, Latter-day Saints worship together as families and in many ways interact with members of all ages and at various stages of spiritual development.

- Mormons attest to the reality of actual historical events as the source of the Church's legitimacy and our gospel understanding. We share this valuing of history with pristine Christianity and perhaps the inception of Islam, quite in contrast to other Christian groups. This attestation is extremely concrete and earthbound and, as Harold Bloom said, "audacious."[6] It invites incredulity but can also forcefully persuade. It poses for everyone a hard but simple challenge: Did it really happen or didn't it?

5. In Paul's words from his letter to the Ephesians, we are, in our congregations, "fellow citizens" in the "household of God," for whom our mutual edification comes from a lay priesthood and complete involvement by all members (Eph. 2:19; 4:12). This edification takes place each Sunday through exhortation and the sacrament, which reinforce our common commitment to Christ and his purposes. We often participate largely from a sense of duty, while perhaps begrudging the

frequent redundancy and long-windedness of our meetings, but it instills toleration and concern for others and does us good.

6. My final reason takes precedence over all the others and is tied again to what we call a testimony. In all religions, the principle of obedience to God is fundamental. If we are potentially glorious, as the Restored Gospel tells us we are, it is also true that we are infinitesimal in the scheme of our Creator's grand universe. This paradox requires that, should we sufficiently believe it, we no longer have a choice about our future. As Muslims so devoutly and sometimes recklessly say, "In sha' All'a!"—"God wills it!" In language the Latter-day Saints are more familiar with, he says, "Be still and know that I am God" (D&C 101:16).

There are, moreover, a number of what I call hooks or promptings that, as I now look back on them, seem to have steered my life in ways I could never have foreseen. These often arose unbidden as invitations or opportunities that required a choice between two alternative courses of action—one leading to greater personal fulfillment, the other to stagnation. I now view such encouragement toward greater activity as God's tender mercies, delivered through the whisperings of his Spirit. I believe this is most often how God operates in our lives.

As a Church patriarch, I've now been privy to that process in the lives of over two thousand Latter-day Saints to whom I have been privileged to give blessings throughout the vast territory of Eastern Europe. Each time I travel abroad on this assignment, I witness the transformation in the lives of those I interview which, as they frequently testify, took place when they acquired a testimony and through the Spirit's transcendent power and their determination to exercise the discipline necessary to change, often dramatically.

Like our convert ancestors, new Church members are

spiritually quickened. Paradoxically, their vital, whole-souled response to the missionaries' message fortifies not only their own lives but those of the missionaries as well. Meanwhile, those in succeeding generations have as much need of that same quickening by overcoming the complacent drag that comes if we assume the whole thing is the mere consequence of family heritage. This applies to all who have mostly just "gone along" with Church teachings and programs.

The human condition spares none of us, nor are our loved ones spared, from discouragement and sorrow, and for those who lack faith in immortality and salvation, the prospect can be utterly grim. There seems to be an innate craving in us for the assurance of Christ's atoning mission. We are therefore truly blessed when, with faith (and despite whatever skeptical arguments also occur to us), we buy into the gospel's assurances and begin to cultivate belief. We have each experienced spiritual nurture and its opposite. I find that living by faith is an immense blessing. I could never allow the sum total of inequities, people's short-sightedness, or the predilections of equally human ecclesiastical mentors to rob me of the gift of being fully open to what Christ offers us.

Paul, again, asserted that we peer "through a glass darkly." Even so, I have at times felt the mind of God that Paul knew contrasts with the mind of man (1 Cor. 2:11-14). I like to call this the epistemology of the gospel. Our faith easily wanes from one moment to the next and from day to day. For me, it has been reassuring to know I can still entertain doubt after the witness I received as a young missionary.

It's humbling and perhaps needful to be reminded of both the finiteness of our physical condition and the limitations of our mortal understanding. There is no proof to the contrary and much to be existentially gained by continuing to trust in Christ's teachings and promises. The equal need of our very loved ones—spouses and children—for spiritual nourishment and an eternal perspective is a key to the endurance required of us in the face of trials.

I consider the Restored Gospel to be distinctively comprehensive and efficacious in meeting our individual and social needs. It is so reasonable in its explication of Judeo-Christianity and so grand in its perspective of our ultimate eternal possibilities that I see it as the essence of humanism and a literal fulfillment of the grand ideal of the fraternity and sisterhood of humankind. Meanwhile, I remain pensive and deeply stirred by Simone Weil's observation that "Instead of speaking about love of truth, it would be better to speak about a spirit of truth in love."[7] I sense such love in many of my fellow Latter-day Saints and would like to do better at emulating them in that regard—or, more specifically, in emulating Jesus's example, which for me will always involve active participation in his Church.

Notes

1. *Huebener* premiered in the fall of 1976 at BYU's Margetts Theater, but Church authorities, fearing repercussions in the German Democratic Republic, requested that we not schedule additional runs of the play. Some considered my compliance with this request to be heroic while others saw it as the opposite. In my mind, my quiet acquiescence reflected nothing so much as a strong preservationist instinct. *Fire in the Bones* premiered in the spring of 1978 at the Greenbriar Theater in Sandy, Utah. It was, to my knowledge, the first literary treatment of the Mountain Meadows Massacre, just as *Huebener* was the first such treatment of the tortured Mormon response to Nazism among native Germans. A revival of *Huebener* was mounted in 1992 at BYU's Pardoe Theater. Both plays were published in *God's Fools: Plays of Mitigated Conscience* and *Huebener and*

The Church was concerned about the message the play, *Huebener*, could send to the German Democratic Republic. Six years later, the Church announced a temple in East Germany, shown here in a detail of the Angel Moroni captured by Wolfgang Thieme in August 2002. © *Corbis Images*

Other Plays; *Fire in the Bones* was re-issued in the 2006 issue of the Association for Mormon Letters publication, *Irreantum*.

2. William Butler Yeats, "The Second Coming." I used this image in a poem, "Limbs," published in *Dialogue: A Journal of Mormon Thought* 14, issue 2 (Summer 1981): 132. During the two and a half years of my first mission, now over fifty years distant, I began to discern the rationalizations people sometimes give for putting off what they know in their hearts is right. I detect that kind of hollow defensiveness in statements by associates when they tell me why they no longer support the Church.

3. At the suggestion of Mr. Kamal, the LDS Church cooperated with the country of Jordan in establishing a Center for Cultural and Educational Affairs in Amman. The center dispenses humanitarian aid to displaced Palestinians and others and arranges student and cultural exchanges between Jordan and the LDS Church, specifically Brigham Young University (see "Global Mormonism Project" online at *Brigham Young University*, http://globalmormonism.byu.edu/).

4. Expressed during a private conversation with the poet.

5. Inscribed on the pedestal of a statue of Mother Teresa in a New Orleans cemetery. These ideas were stimulated through a wonderful conversation with another former student, Sterling Van Wagenen.

6. Harold Bloom, "The Religion-Making Imagination of Joseph Smith," *The American Religion* (New York: Touchstone Books, 1992), 99.

7. Cited in Richard Rees, *Simone Weil: A Sketch for a Portrait* (Carbondle: Southern Illinois University Press, 1966), 152.

On the Lord's Errand

Cherry Bushman Silver

I grew up during the Second World War in Portland, Oregon, where our family was part of the out-migration from Utah. We Bushman children learned to value and defend our peculiar religion in a high school where only a dozen others were Church members. It was a major event when my brother Richard was elected student body president. We accepted being peculiar as a commitment. Living the Church standards was something worth defending.

When the missionaries brought two new girls to the Mutual Improvement Association, all the young members became involved in befriending them. We felt pride in our beliefs when the girls investigated and then embraced the LDS gospel. At their baptism I felt a goodness. That good feeling has been a fundamental part of my Church life.

Vigorous and enlightened gospel discussions increased when my family returned to Salt Lake City in 1950. I was in high school and college during the years of the Oscar Hunter firesides on Sunday evenings in the Bonneville Stake, an informal group of young people preparing for missions who explored topics under a dynamic discussant. In the summers and on holidays, we had gatherings of Harvard and Stanford students in our home because my brothers attended those universities. We felt free to examine every Church practice and gospel question from the point of view of faithful inquiry. We lived in a part of town near many of the Church's general authorities, and I had chances to shake hands with presidents of the Church. After living on the fringes, I now felt content being at the center.

My continuing exploration of Mormonism's dynamic theology continued at the University of Utah where I took classes at the LDS Institute of Religion from such effective teachers as Lowell Bennion, T. Edgar Lyon, and George Boyd. During this time I heard the notable debate between Hugh Nibley and Sterling McMurrin. My friends and I valued the ennobling principles found in Latter-day Saint teachings and tried to defend them against attacks.

For graduate work I studied at Boston University and Harvard/Radcliffe, where I attended the Cambridge Branch. Truman Madsen taught Institute classes and George Albert Smith Jr. was a Gospel Doctrine teacher, in whose class we debated ethics during the era of civil rights activism. When the Boston stake was organized, I was called as the stake Young Women's president, helping encourage young people in the small wards around the area.

With my marriage to Barnard Silver in 1963, I detoured from academic interests in order to follow the career of my engineer husband. For twenty-five years we lived in small towns serving sugar beet and cane factories. Our daughter was a toddler when we moved to Lahaina, Maui; she started grade school in Santa Maria, California; and she finished sixth grade in Ferkessédougou, Cote d'Ivoire (Ivory Coast), where we lived for two and a half years. Our son attended first and second grades in Africa and learned to read and write French before English. Both children finished high school in Moses

Lake, Washington, and went on to college, she to Wellesley and he to Harvard.

In Africa our two children were the first Caucasians in the village school, and since we were the only Latter-day Saint family in the country, we held Church services in our living room on the sugar plantation and sent our tithing to Church headquarters through the International Mission. Sunday mornings we invited neighboring black and Creole children to attend meetings in our home and learn the teachings of Christ. We formed a small plantation youth choir for Christmas, and I organized women into a prototype Relief Society for cultural refinement lessons. This was in the mid-1970s before the revelation that gave blacks the priesthood, but we still answered questions from our neighbors about the Church and LDS life, leaving them copies of the Book of Mormon in French. We were doing our best to establish a little Zion in this outpost.

Twelve years later in 1988, we were called to open the Latter-day Saint mission to the Cote d'Ivoire, which was thrilling for Barnard and me as we returned remembering our former friendships and eager to share the gospel with the people of Africa. I will never forget when Philip Assard, a black high priest and first counselor in the unit presidency, administered a blessing of health to Barnard. What a happy reversal of former roles, black hands on a white head, made possible after decades of prayer by current revelation.

Before we began our mission, Elder Alexander Morrison advised us to adopt four traits to avoid being taken advantage of and to keep us, in our naïveté, from ruining the work. "Be bold, courageous, adaptable, and shrewd," he said. That proved to be good advice in the Côte d'Ivoire and also in Zaire, now the Democratic Republic of the Congo, where we were transferred because of security reasons. In our first week in Kinshasa, we were stopped by a squad of soldiers

African women are industrious, independent, and graceful, carrying the burdens of their culture with stoicism and practicality. Here a woman walks to market in Abidjan, Côte d'Ivoire, in a photograph by Zhao Yingguan of Xinhua Press. © *Corbis Images*

who wanted our car, money, and perhaps our lives. That was indeed a challenge to our stock of courage and shrewdness.

One soldier pulled up the door lock, then several of them piled into the car. As one of them grabbed my two-way radio, another fought Barnard for the car keys. A third soldier tried to strangle Barnard to make him loosen his grip on the key in the ignition. They ransacked my handbag but miraculously, even though there were bills there, did not find the money. The squad chief demanded that we open the trunk. Barnard would not until they radioed their commanding officer to come. Then we waited, resistant hostages, declaring that we were American missionaries and would not drive the car off the road and into their stronghold.

During that wait the thought entered my head that while I was on the Lord's errand, I might be asked to give my life and that this might be the end. The soldiers could rough us up. They could put us in one of their notorious jails. They could seize our car and dump our bodies in the river. But I felt calm, believing we were part of the sweep of history and the swift ascendency of gospel influence in Africa. If the Lord needed us to survive, he would help. I had committed to be there despite discomfort and danger. And for what? For the joy of interacting with people who were making core decisions about their futures, perhaps helping them change small pieces of their world as prompted by the Holy Spirit.

When the commander arrived a half-hour later, his tone was less aggressive than that of the local soldiers. He saw that we were not candidates for a bribe. We opened the trunk of the car and shared part of its treasure with the soldiers—pamphlets in French telling the Joseph Smith story—but kept our copies of the Book of Mormon for serious investigators. They gave us back the radio, my handbag, and our freedom and sent us on our way.

I stay in the Church because this is the only way of life

that seems real to me. It demands a lot from its members, but it offers benefits in enriching our lives in untold ways. It meshes with my view of God and humankind.

Four principles underlie my philosophy of the Church:

1. From my earliest days, I have felt a fulfilling inner spiritual life. I have felt that God is my father and needs me to do his work. Although I follow my own reasoning and instincts, I sense a constant guiding hand. I see miracles in the world each day and every week. I believe that God is serious and does not allow us to violate his order of things with impunity. So I respect the institutions he has established and the leaders he has called. On the other hand, I feel as if I can talk to him with candor, in an intimate way as one of his children.

2. The Church provides a structure through which we work with others for community uplift, for fellowship, and for learning. Within the Church, my ambition has not simply been to follow the Church leaders, but to contribute my own thoughts and efforts. Serving on the general board of the Relief Society and on the General Committee for Members with Disabilities in the 1990s provided me with an unusual chance to do this not only with women leaders but also with our advisors, the Seventies and Apostles.

3. I see this life through the lenses of pragmatism and irony. All institutions in this world have flaws. My worldview envisions a Father in Heaven who gives us an understanding of our human condition but who does not disclose more information than we can make use of. I think he operates, as we do, in a world of choices where the contest between good and evil requires our active participation. He lends his power and perspectives, but in my view the details are not predestined.

4. For me, membership in the Church adds zest to life. I value exploring ideas with fellow believers, those acquainted with the terms and issues of Mormondom who have a sense of what is genuinely at stake. I respect what our parents and

ancestors have contributed. I am presently trying to reconstruct the social and spiritual milieu of earlier believing Saints through the editing of the Emmeline B. Wells diaries. I am impressed by the intensity of their commitment to the Church even as they lived under tremendous political and social pressures.

These days Barnard and I teach Sunday School at the Utah State Prison. We talk with men who ask the ultimate questions of life. Among the marginalized people there, we find a centrality of faith and hope. Many of them acquire a spirit of charity with regard to those around them, which is wonderful to see. We feel grateful that the Church provides strong programs for people in all circumstances, that at the prison, for instance, inmates can participate in the Church's family history library, a music school, and Institute classes, as well as counseling and worship services.

I can see how we all, whether we live on the outskirts or at the center of the Church, may build better lives through this remarkable institution. The Church teaches me to rely on the Redeemer and strengthen my personal witness of his grace. It provides me with a sense of purpose and a zest for life that transcends every other way of living that I know of. I have found both freedom and fulfillment here and am very pleased to be caught in the gospel net.

Heartfelt Moments and Learning Experiences

William Bradshaw

I remain an active, committed member of the LDS Church. I do so because I want to keep singing the songs, especially the children's songs with lyrics that ring true and meaningfully in my grandfatherhood. I want to remember the feeling in the room as Bryan, my son-in-law, held his autistic son in his arms and lowered the apprehensive child gently into the baptismal font. I want to retain some of the insights that have come, for example, during the period when I timed what people in my ward said in fast and testimony meeting. The data are clear. The average length of an adult testimony is 4.5 minutes, and 2 percent of the congregation, the five regulars, occupy 45 percent of the time. Children's testimonies average 22 seconds including transit time. With important exceptions, I am moved most often by two-minute expressions of people aged fourteen through twenty. They tend to be unrehearsed, unpolished sentiments, delivered haltingly, with repetition of phrases such as "like … you know" and an honest "I'm not sure it's true," along with the heartfelt, "I hope it is." At these times I am reminded of my mission and the uncertain, groping first prayers of investigators who, not having been taught how to pray, somehow do so in the way prayer was intended.

There are Mormons whose company I want to retain. One of them is Marion "Duff" Hanks, who was my teachers quorum adviser before he came to prominence in the Church. I cannot recall specific words spoken during those hours with him, but he told stories of people whose lives were commendable, how they behaved in time of war and in the face of other challenges. I came to believe what he was telling me was true; he had a way of talking that made me pay attention. Over the years when he was a general authority, I never fell asleep during his conference addresses. Years later as a mission president, I saw firsthand the power of this good man's words. I sat listening as a troubled young Mormon soldier poured out his heart. The place was Tan Son Nhut airbase in Saigon. His platoon had been on patrol in the jungle and his best friend, who had been on point, took an AK47 round to his head and lay dying in the hospital as we spoke. I was quiet, attentive, as the words tumbled out. The Mormon boy had no shirt, his hair was long, beads and peace symbols hung from his neck, and he was hanging on to the Church by his fingertips. Two older brothers had left the military dishonorably. His slender conduit to sanity was a girlfriend in St. George. She had sent the *Ensign* with the conference reports and he had read and responded to Duff's sermon, whose message was inclusive of those at the margins of the Church. I fumbled to confirm that Duff was right and encouraged the young man to keep hanging on.

At a number of times in my life, I have been the recipient of selfless service in fulfillment of the injunction to "comfort those in need of comfort." Such goodness is not exclusive to Mormons, but of those with whom I have experienced such generosity, a significant number have been Latter-day Saints. And I also stay because of my heritage, because of those who came before me to whom I am indebted, because of sacrifices of which I am only dimly aware but which have made my life and faith possible.

Among those I would like to meet in the next life, should the opportunity come, would be my paternal grandfather. We never encountered each other in life. George Hampson Bradshaw was born in St. Louis in 1857. His immigrant family had converted to Mormonism in Manchester, England, in the 1840s. His uncles worked in the coal mines near St. Louis as the family accumulated enough for the trek west. After a short stop in Nebraska where a younger brother was born, the Bradshaws arrived in Salt Lake City in 1862 and at Maughn's Fort (renamed Wellsville) in Cache Valley in 1864. There was very little of food and shelter, but they had an ample supply of hard work, cold weather, and sometimes unfriendly Native Americans. In 1896, with a wife, three children, and a labor-intensive farm to maintain, George accepted a mission call to Great Britain. One experience there stands out for me. While speaking at a street meeting at Speaker's Corner in Hyde Park in London, he was repeatedly challenged by a heckler in the crowd with, "Where's Balaam's ass?" (Num. 22). The missionary's response: "I think I hear him braying in the congregation!" I'm reasonably sure that that segment of my DNA which influences a sense of humor came from my Grandpa George, and I'm looking forward to a time when I might be able to trade quips with him.

In addition to past history, I have been influenced in my thinking by important things that have happened directly to me. I'll share two from my college days. The bedroom of Straus House at Harvard where I spent my college freshman year was on the ground floor. The back wall was only feet from where people emerged from the subway into Harvard Square. It was small, and as I was the last of the four roommates to arrive, I acquired the default position on the top of the bunk bed. Sleeping on the bottom bunk was Al Grossman who was from New York City and was extremely bright. He had a wry smile and alternately smoked a pipe and cigarettes. I stayed up late studying a lot that year.

One early Sunday morning was particularly memorable because I was at my desk in the outer room between two and three in the morning, my paper still unfinished, when Al returned inebriated, suspended unsteadily between two friends. He waved cheerily and was carried to our room and dropped into oblivion on his mattress. Of course, the kid from Utah was appalled. I finished a couple of hours later and decided I could get three or four hours' sleep before walking to priesthood meeting. I opened the bedroom door and was even more disgusted. Al had recycled everything from his earlier revelry. It was everywhere, vile and putrid. I closed the door and my righteous indignation soared. How dare he? He should be keeping the World of Wisdom like me. He should be honorable and good like me. I wasn't sure what produced the change in me, but after a while I went back in the room and, armed with every towel from the bathroom, cleaned it all up: the floor, the sheets, and Al himself, still dead to the world and grinning as I wiped his face. A few hours later it would be for me a sobering, less judgmental fifteen-minute walk along Brattle Street to the chapel. The meetings that day were somehow different and so was I. Parents send their children to Brigham Young University where I now teach, hoping they'll never have to experience a night like that. However, I am deeply, profoundly grateful that it happened to me and that I could learn that there might be reasons to transcend moral judgment.

Another night on the top bunk in that same bedroom, I started, by choice, to read the Book of Mormon. Feeling from previous efforts that I was an expert in the goodliness of Nephi's parentage, I forged ahead to the next verse and then beyond to where Nephi recounted his father's death. I am unable to adequately convey the impact that those words had on me. How could someone so precisely describe my own feelings? What was the source of the power in those words? Straus House will always be an important place for me, and I believe, now as then, that it is the Savior to whom I am indebted for what happened there.

And so I stay in the Church because of what I have come to believe about revelation. I could be wrong, but I believe the mechanics of the revelatory process are the same for all of us at any level of Church membership and that our decisions, both trivial and grave, reflect in some measure our unperfected humanity, weaknesses, and ignorance as we inevitably fall short of the ideal. We are all wrong about some issues, and none of us can be relieved of the obligation to be tolerant and patient as we peer darkly through the glass of individual perspective and listen to the voice inside of us that can guide us to a better path.

At the end of 1972, the U.S. government announced the termination of our military involvement in Vietnam. As mission president, I started to receive inquiries from Church headquarters about what I proposed to do in order to continue our operations in that country. Everyone was worried about security there. In March 1973 I made what could have been my last trip to Saigon. During that visit I went to the Caravelle Hotel, took the elevator to the top floor restaurant, exited to the roof, and climbed the stairs to the top of the building. The view across the flat expanse of the Mekong Delta from that site is impressive. I could see many of the major landmarks of the city. Elder Gordon B. Hinckley had offered a dedicatory prayer in that building several years before. I also sought inspiration as to how we should proceed in a country still at war. I cannot truly reproduce in words the nature of that experience but will say that I felt an intense

"The view across the flat expanse of the Mekong Delta" from the top of the Caravelle Hotel in Saigon (now Ho Chi Minh City) "is impressive." The hotel is shown here as it appeared on Christmas Eve, 1966, from the Bettmann Archive. © *Corbis Images*

sense of my prayer being answered. I returned to the hotel with serenity and comfort about what the future would bring. Upon returning to Hong Kong, I wrote to Elder Hinckley recommending that we assign full-time missionaries to Vietnam. That request was granted. It was implemented when I brought four elders from Hong Kong to Saigon on April 6, 1973.

The withdrawal of the U.S. military from South Vietnam and the introduction of full-time missionaries brought changes to the Church there, including a reorganization of the Saigon branch presidency. Our experience in Hong Kong made it clear that progress would be more likely if local priesthood leaders were given administrative authority and expatriates and missionaries assumed a more secondary role. With that in mind, Nguyen Van The was called to be the branch president, with Dang Thong Nhat as first counselor and Lester Bush as second counselor. The day I set these men apart was particularly significant for me and remains so today.

My ecclesiastical position at the time provided frequent occasion to perform an ordinance mediated through the laying on of hands for priesthood ordinations and setting apart to positions of responsibility in the Church. I believe I made an honest attempt on each occasion to seek inspiration for the words that I spoke. But what happened when I set Lester apart was out of the ordinary. I regard it as sacred and believe that deity influenced the content of what was said and the manner in which it was pronounced. It was a humbling experience. The maintenance and growth of the Church in Vietnam during that time was due in large measure to the efforts of Lester and his wife, Yvonne, two truly exceptional Latter-day Saints.

Another reason why I stay in the Church is because others whom I love are members. Of all I could write about spiritually affirming experiences, none is so personal, intimate, and important as those involving my wife, Marge, and our children. Five times we have held hands across a hospital bed before and after cesarian surgeries. Nothing else seems to matter as you plead with God while your sweetheart is undergoing the risks of bringing children into the world. And of course, the anxiety continues after they get here. In Seattle our oldest, Bill, only five years old, required repeated procedures to repair a retinal detachment. "Doesn't matter," he told his mother as she tried to adjust the holes in the Batman mask she had made to fit over his eyes, "I can't see with that eye anyway."

In Oak Ridge, Tennessee, Bart, also five, had ridden his bike down the driveway of a home across the street right into the path of an oncoming car. He suffered a compound fracture and lay in traction in the hospital for two days before his leg could be placed in a cast. Sometime during this painful interval the doctor asked, "Well, what do you want to be when you grow up?" "Just a dad," our son replied as if that were the greatest thing in the world.

In Hong Kong there was another car accident when Brett, age seven, was struck by a hit-and-run driver while crossing the street to a popsicle vender. An off-duty policeman took him to the Baptist Hospital at the end of the block. A call from the nurses alerted us to what had happened. His spleen was ruptured and the good physician held the fractured organ in his hand while a search was made for O-negative blood needed for a transfusion. It is not a common blood type among the Chinese. A single pint was finally located, which we were able to replace through a lady missionary's generosity. We made it through these trials in no small part because of the faith that the Church had taught us to strive for. These three boys, now men, are doing well. I see myself as having rung up a huge debt to God.

I stay in spite of grievances I harbor, including having to

listen to a brother give a priesthood lesson and say, "Why, even in *our* Republican Party, we occasionally make a mistake." "Mistake, thy name is legion," I mutter under my breath. Or hearing from the pulpit condemnation of working mothers unable to greet their children returning from school with just-baked cookies. Or recitation of the near-canonical explanation that BYU professors only teach evolution so the school won't lose its accreditation. They don't know they are talking about me. If you believe I might be made of such stern stuff that I don't rant and rave about these things on the way home from Church, you would be wrong. You may not be aware of the serious internal turmoil I nearly always feel when I notice *The Proclamation on the Family* mounted on the wall of a home I'm visiting and remember how often in a Church setting that document is used to justify erroneous statements, insensitivity, and un-Christian remarks or behavior toward my homosexual brothers and sisters.

I stay despite having issues with practices and policies. In the fall of 1997, I wrote the following letter to the director of the fine arts museum at BYU after learning the sculpture, *The Kiss,* would be removed from an exhibition at the university of Rodin's work. In subsequent semesters I would reread it in other classes while projecting on a screen a photograph of myself standing next to the original work in Paris.

> I read this statement to the students in my cell biology class today. I've been quite troubled over the past several days. Since my job at this institution is to profess, I'd like to do that for the next two minutes. What you will hear is an individual point of view, and is not intended to represent my faculty colleagues or my department or college. During the 15 months I was on sabbatical leave in Boston two and one half years ago, my assignment in the Belmont Ward was to teach the seven-year-old CTR

[Choose the Right] class in Primary. It was a great time for me. I am reminded of it on occasion when I see a CTR ring on one of your fingers. It is because I believe in choosing the right, and because promoting that decision-making process is a major function of a university that I am both saddened and angry about a decision that prevents you from seeing and enjoying some of the world's great art. The three brief points I want to make are about choosing.

First, I have seen some of Rodin's work in a wonderful outdoor patio at Stanford, and have a strong sense of the positive, ennobling spirit that it carries. I believe all of you ought to be making distinctions between love and lasciviousness, between the lewd and the lovely, and shun that which is pornographic. But this is not a close call. Second, I think the Church is hurt by what has happened. It is my opinion that a significant number of people who might otherwise have agreed to listen to the missionaries decided this week not to. For them the unfortunate stereotype of us as narrow-minded and unreasonable has been reinforced. At the protest yesterday one woman held a sign whose sensible message is worth repeating: "It's O.K. to be a peculiar people; we don't have to be a ridiculous people." Three, one justification offered for keeping these statues from our view is that some museum visitors might be offended—the young school child or the spinster from Lehi or the Stake President from Orange County, California—all with tender sensibilities. Why, then, show these works? Because this is a university and everyone should know that we are in the business of helping people use their minds more effectively so that they'll be able to choose the right. Come to BYU and we'll help you understand the distinction between the great and the trivial or trashy in art. Why show these works? Because we've been teaching you since you were seven to choose the right, no matter what anyone else in the world thinks about it—even the well-intentioned sister from Lehi who believes there's no place for a representation of people who aren't wearing clothes.

One event that saved my day yesterday, and every day, is to go home—leaving a cluttered office piled with unfinished work—and receive a tender, sometimes passionate kiss from my wife. That is not an improper or immoral experience. In fact, it's absolutely marvelous, and if you have that kind of a relationship with someone, I recommend it highly. I further recommend that after you leave Provo, if you ever get a second change to see Rodin's "The Kiss," you should take it. In my opinion you'll be choosing the right.

Finally, I stay because I promised that I would. Looking back, I'm pretty sure there was a time as a Latter-day Saint when, though I didn't know everything, I thought I could handle the great questions about faith. Moreover, I probably unconsciously assumed that whatever uncertainties I had would diminish with age and experience. I was wrong. Now I find myself in the very paradoxical state of being less sure about a whole lot of things, but having greater faith. I'm not sure why that's true. I used to view the statement, "Have faith in Christ," as an injunction that "you'd better have faith or else." Now I see it as a simple description of the way things are, the way this life works. There is no alternative. I am not going to be relieved anytime soon of the need for faith, especially in Him. I feel even more strongly that I'm going to keep the commitments I've made to a fairly large number of people, beginning with those I love the most, my wife, Marge, and our children and grandchildren, and extending to a lot of young people who have entrusted something of their minds and hearts to me over the years. I believe that Jesus will reciprocate with a vote of confidence and patience as I try to make sense of the world around me as best I can.

Everything I Ever Needed to Know I Learned in Church

Claudia L. Bushman

I don't want to explore why I stay in the Church. I just don't like that question. Of course I have had some pretty horrific experiences that would have persuaded many to leave. I could give a very salty talk about putdowns I have experienced and insults I have borne. I have been publicly and privately humiliated on several occasions. And if I went into any details at all, I am sure you would agree that I have been treated very badly and have every right to shake the dust of Zion from my shoes. But I have forgiven those perpetrators. I cannot say that I have forgotten the slights. Instead I have adopted the style of various Church leaders that I have known. They may forgive, but they never forget.

My raw wounds have faded some with time. And I am certainly not alone among those who have suffered at the hands of our leaders. I have observed lots of such experiences in the Church and watched with sorrow as some people I know and love have finally announced their unwillingness to bear the final straw and left. I don't think they are any happier or better off without the Church.

My question is not why I stay in the Church, but why should I leave? I love the Church. I don't want to leave it. My

Church experience is deeply ingrained. It may come before my identity as a woman. It certainly comes before my identity as an American. My grandparents came from four different countries and, caught up in the gospel net, left their homes and families and came to a new place, forging new families and connections. None of them ever left the Church. None ever returned to their previous homes. They remained faithful to the end, as did my parents. The Church was the mixing bowl that brought them together and the mold that shaped their lives. During bad times, and they suffered some very bad ones, it was all in all to them. They were great people within their own spheres, devoted to the gospel, and to them I owe a heavy debt that I currently pay on whenever I can. I don't ever want to compromise their steadiness and sacrifice. They pointed the direction to a way of life, a purpose, and an identity. Thank heavens for that.

Besides that, I personally owe a great debt to the Church. Look what the Church provides. A community wherever you go. An arena for participation to do whatever you want and a cadre of the best and most willing workers in the world. The Church gives you a sense of where you are, to borrow the memorable statement of Bill Bradley, the great basketball player. It gives you purchase on your life. You see things in context.

One of my first memories is of standing before a large group at Christmastime, singing "O Hush Thee My Baby, A Story I'll Tell." I had my little rubber doll wrapped in a dish towel and I rocked her as I sang, completely caught up in the feeling of Christmas, unafraid, singing to my brothers and sisters as I had been taught to do. Mormons are the most tolerant of audiences. We are all part of the group and as we dispense good feeling and kindness, we can expect acceptance and approval in return. I spent my youth in that protected globe where good feelings were so generously dispersed.

When I attended my fiftieth high school reunion a few years back, one of my old friends surprised me by saying that I was the only person in the class who seemed to have any idea of what I was doing, that I knew that something came after high school. What a blessing not to be dependent on the values and approvals of my beautiful, much-loved but crazy high school class. They really did not have a clue. Thanks to the Church, I lived in the alternative universe of San Francisco's Sunset Ward as well as in the dispensation of the fullness of times. I had a little purchase on life.

The Church provided me with a perfect school. Everything I ever needed to know I learned in Church. Not only did I learn a large share of songs and finger plays in Primary, I learned to give talks, be in programs and plays, respond politely and warmly when I was spoken to, sing parts, and learned the tango (many times). I learned how to sing thousands of songs, conduct a meeting, organize an outing.

Because I gave lots of talks, I was able to organize and carry forward uncounted school and civic projects and do a good deal of community service. Because I have been in hundreds of musical presentations, I can lead a choir and put on a pretty good presentation of my own. Because I was president of little Primary groups, I learned how to manage big programs and have carried on many since. Like many Church workers, I specialize in making something out of not much.

The Church provides myriads of communities. Once in graduate school I was talking to a friend. She said she was sad, that she felt lonely and alone in the universe. I told her that I sometimes felt that way. She said that I could not possibly understand as I had the Mormons. Of course, she was right. I never will really feel that way because I always do have the Mormons. I can find friends anywhere. I already have friends everywhere. I have a community to belong to in any place I go to. I can visit with the elders on the street. I can find people who are recognizably Mormon, who know people I know even if I don't know them to begin with. I can start a conversation and have instant intimacy in no time. We have lived in three cities, in three wards, during the last year. We have dear friends in all of them.

What I most value about the Church is the way we create our congregations and carry on our Church business. We have leaders and manuals and traditions, but we are still on our own, creating our classes and relationships, each congregation with its own character, its own strengths and weaknesses, each of us with a place in it, if we wish to occupy one. We have a built-in group of friends if we choose to take them up. We don't have to interact with all those people all the time, but we can if we want to.

What else do I like? I love the way the Church is an arena for all the kinds of projects I want to do. I am a project person. I get it from my mother and my grandmother who were always doing projects. My mother would get an idea and then cajole her brothers and sisters to help her bring it to fruition. And it wasn't too hard to get them to do that as she could personify charm itself and because she had taken them through many delightful events, programs, and other activities in the past. The Mormon people are a dream to work with, so cooperative, so willing, usually so dependable, so reliable. They've all been through the same boot camp, learning how to do things, learning how to say yes instead of no, learning how to support and serve others. I love to work with Mormons. They know how to do it. Nobody does it better.

One of my daughters-in-law had a living nativity scene with the neighbors every Christmas when her children were young. It was the usual manger scene with scriptures read and songs sung, the Holy Family, the shepherds and the kings in costume. She discovered very early that the neighboring kids could not sing. They had never learned how. She had to salt her groups with Primary kids who could carry tunes and who knew Christmas songs. There is just no substitute for the Saints. Nobody works or cooperates the way they do.

A few years back when the Manhattan Temple was under construction, we began work on our youth jubilee. We had a group of 2,500 young people from fifteen or so distant stakes. We had the largest cast that had ever appeared on the stage of Radio City Music Hall, a thrilling, if venerable, venue where it is very difficult to get on and off stage. We had only one day in the theatre, the performance day. The professional staff said that there was no way in the world that we could put on a show like that with volunteer labor. But of course we did, and it was a great show, sharp, tight, entertaining, and as our frugal President Hinckley who attended said, "worth every penny." I was so high after this thrilling experience that I would have trekked to Nauvoo on my knees if anyone had suggested it.

In working together, we become family. I love the people I work with. We become rich in fellow feeling, even as we accomplish some pretty good things. And working together is the ultimate lesson we learn: not to accomplish the task, but to work together; not to sulk, not to rise to anger, not to walk out, but to work together. And that's one of the reasons I forgive the slights of insensitive leaders. They have just forgotten that our highest aim is to learn to work together. We are to love one another, treat each other with respect, and work peaceably together.

We are fortunate to have such an interesting Church structure, such colorful doctrines, such tortured relationships with other Churches and individuals. All this has been cast in bright relief during recent years with the anniversary of the Mountain Meadows Massacre, the death of our ninety-seven-year-old prophet, the Romney and Huntsman candidacies, the Tony-award-winning *The Book of Mormon.* It is so interesting to see what people think of us and to attempt to negotiate those relationships. I am so glad not to be anything ordinary in the religious line, but to have a history, beliefs, and activities that leave others incredulous, amazed, horrified, bewildered, even as they find our people square, ingenuous, remarkably successful, and too good to be true. We can prepare some very interesting answers to questions on religious matters.

I don't consider myself a very good person. I tend to be snide, cynical, and critical. I have never managed to be the good sweet girl I was taught to be at Church. It's all part of my left-handed, depressed psyche. I could very well be a bitter hermit. I could be one of those who is poisoned by her own gall. I could be a very unhappy person. But I'm not. I'm sociable, friendly, and warm. I know that people rely on me and I rely on them. I am interested in what they are doing. Our Church experience is full of wonderful relationships.

So I have given a number of reasons why I do not intend to leave the Church, listed things that the Church has done for me. But important as those are to me, as grateful as I am for my experiences, these are not the most important reasons I would give. Why don't I leave the Church? Because I think the Church needs me.

The Church needs people who can speak the language of the outsider and explain things that are otherwise inexplicable. The Church needs her intellectuals, people who can talk to secular thinkers who dismiss Mormonism, and not be ruffled. The Church needs people who have learned the Church's lessons and can teach them to the next generation, who can run things and carry projects along. The Church needs older people who are willing to occupy the outposts of society, to go on missions, to take part in community activities, to demonstrate the wonderful service we so often direct inwardly.

The Church needs people, particularly women, who speak out in frank ways during lessons and discussions, to give courage to those who have things to say but do not dare to say them. The Church needs people who, having had more experience, don't give the pat answers. The Church needs older women who do more than sit in their rocking chairs and quilt.

I don't want to add to the statistics of the angered, the offended, the disillusioned. This is my Church. This is my life. So why would I even think of leaving the Church? I'm happy here. I certainly hope and pray that the Church does not decide to leave me.

Living Indefinitely with Ambiguity

Armand L. Mauss

In some ways, I find the question of why I stay with the Church to be peculiar. No one asks me why I stay with my family or with my nation, both of which connections are periodically stressful and no less voluntary than my relationship to the Church. The implicit question behind the explicit one is slightly different: Why *should* we stay? From my perspective as a life-long Church member, the question is rather revealing if somewhat troubling, especially as a recurring question at the Sunstone Symposium; for it suggests that it is a salient, and perhaps pervasive, question among the most recent generations of Church members. If this is so, it indicates the failure of the Church, perhaps on a large scale, to provide enough answers to that implicit question despite half a century in which more young people than ever before have grown up with high-school-age seminary classes, college-age Institute of Religion classes, and attendance at Brigham Young University. Having grown up in California during the early days of the Mormon diaspora, I had access to none of these programs of instruction and indoctrination, and yet I have stayed. Indeed, I have never contemplated leaving. Why not? Perhaps only because I am a stubborn old man unwilling to concede that I could have been wrong all these years! Yet, I think there is more to be said.

As our late beloved colleague Eugene England taught us, we should reject the cliché that it is the gospel, rather than the Church, that is truly important.[1] I love the gospel, insofar as I can understand it. I would continue trying to abide by its teachings whether or not I stayed with the Church—a position apparently shared by some of my friends and colleagues who no longer go to Church. My acceptance of the gospel of Jesus Christ, as taught in the Latter-day Saint tradition, is a matter of choice rather than empirical certainty. I have my doubts. I always have had and always will. I think doubt is the inescapable companion of serious, reflective thought. I make no apologies for my doubts or for choosing to believe in spite of them. Still, the Church is where we are reminded weekly of what's right and how to put our beliefs into action. It is where we teach our children. It is where we support each other and engage in acts of charity. It is where we learn to tolerate each other's idiosyncrasies. It is also in Church where we struggle with our doubts and strive to make peace with them.

Contrary to what many skeptics and atheists would suggest, it is common for human beings to hold to assumptions that are never empirically tested or that, indeed, never can be. In the jargon of science, these beliefs and assumptions are "unfalsifiable," and they are not all religious in nature. For instance, Freudian psychology generally, and psychoanalysis in particular, are based on assumptions that cannot be tested even though they are widely applied in therapy. Similarly, predictions of any kind about the future cannot be tested or falsified ahead of time but must be taken on faith whether the future in question is in the next world, or the physical environment of this world, or the nation's economy. My own unfalsifiable beliefs and assumptions are therefore as valid as the next person's, but they are mine. Yet so much in the gospel, as in the secular world, is subject to the test of experience, at least on an individual basis, if not always replicable in universal experience. Having long since entered my ninth decade of mortality, my experiences have taught me the wisdom of trying to live by gospel principles, sometimes through the setbacks and unhappiness I have experienced–and caused others–during times when I have ignored or resisted gospel teachings.

Among the LDS teachings, I am particularly intrigued by the innovative ideas of the prophet Joseph Smith, especially those regarded as most unorthodox by other Christians. I continue to find his ideas engaging and prophetic. Of course, there are some doctrines in both Christianity and Mormonism that I don't understand very well; however, I do not experience these as nagging doubts or problems but rather as challenges. I have come to understand that living indefinitely with ambiguity is a sign of intellectual maturity, not weakness. For example, I don't understand the logic behind the atonement of the Savior. I don't worry about it, though, since the only thing I need to understand in this life is that the atonement is applicable to me only as I live the principle of repentance. Otherwise, it has no efficacy, no matter how well or how little I understand it. Learning to repent is a good policy for all of us, whatever theological rationale we give it. Similarly, there is a lot about the temple and genealogy that I find difficult to assimilate. Yet the eternal efficacy of temple marriage, for example, seems more likely if the parties have made a formal covenant for eternity than if they are married explicitly only for *this* life, as is the case outside the LDS temple. Vicarious work too, whatever its eternal significance might turn out to be, seems at least to foster family bonds in the here and now—to turn the hearts of the fathers and children toward each other, as the scripture says. So I do my family history research and take my turn at temple assignments whenever they come along.

My outlook on the Church, however, is a different matter

from my religious beliefs, however well I might have rationalized those beliefs. My understanding of the history and operation of the Church derive from academic study as well as from experience. My background in sociology allows me the kind of detached scholarly perspective necessary to understand and appreciate the Church as an essentially human institution. As a matter of personal belief, I am convinced that Joseph Smith had a number of encounters with Deity or the supernatural. I don't subscribe exactly to the official historical accounts of those encounters, but because of them I attribute a divine origin to the Church. At the same time, my sociological perspective and study have convinced me that the Church, whatever its origins, is not immune to the human processes and natural historical developments common to all social institutions. In other words, despite its divine origin, the Church has, throughout its history, functioned mainly as a human institution with divine intervention difficult to ascertain and probably rare. I have found this perspective helpful to my attitude toward the Church and to my emotional well-being generally. Since I expect the Church usually to operate as a human institution, and its leaders as human beings, I am occasionally disappointed but never disillusioned.

The admonition "follow the prophet" is given with increasing frequency in the Church. In many ways it is wise counsel, and I accept it as a general rule. However, it is often transformed into a ritualistic slogan or mantra intended to stifle questions and differences of opinion, or else to override the agency of a Church member seeking the direct counsel of the Holy Spirit for individual circumstances. The related folk maxim that "obedience is the first law of heaven" does not accord with a reasonable reading of the scriptural account of the war in heaven where clearly agency was established prior to obedience among the laws on which our Plan of Salvation operates. When such slogans and maxims are employed for leverage by overzealous leaders, contrary to the counsel about "unrighteous dominion" (D&C 121), then the Church operates like any other human institution and is entitled only to the same presumption of qualified loyalty that we give other human institutions. I have sometimes wrestled with my conscience in trying to decide what obedience requires in specific cases including political controversies. Yet, I have never, at least in my adult life, been disillusioned by the counsel of Church leaders with which I have disagreed, or even by the most egregious examples of unrighteous dominion. My understanding of human institutions and how they work has provided me with a kind of immunity to disillusionment.

This is not to say that I don't care about how the Church operates or what happens to it. My sociological detachment doesn't reach that far! I would like to see the Church, as a human institution, also become a bit more *humane.* With divine origins and a divine mandate to bless the world, I would like to see the Church grow and prosper and do much better at retaining members indefinitely, rather than until they become disillusioned. If the Church is the most important repository of truth on the earth, then I would like to see more candor and transparency about the *facts* as well as the *truths* in our own doctrine and history and less defensiveness about the anomalies, even when they are embarrassing. The Church cannot prosper and retain the loyalty of its members if they come through its religious education programs unduly sheltered from our controversies in history and doctrine; for sooner or later, their ignorance will make them vulnerable to the one-sided anti-Mormon claim that they have been lied to.

One of the reasons, then, that I stay in the Church is so that I can contribute to the mitigation of these problems in our big Mormon family. I hasten to add that I do not think of myself as a reformer. That is not my job. However, I am reasonably well informed and have a certain degree of expertise in how organizations can best work toward the achievement of their most important goals. I sometimes make my observations and analyses publicly and in print, for whatever they might be worth, without attempting to "counsel the Brethren" or to criticize them for any inadequacies that I see. I know that some of them listen to me and read what I write, which they might not do if I were just another disillusioned and critical carper.

Another reason I stay is because, at a local level, my ward provides me with a community in which I can make use of the talents and wisdom I have, whether in formal ways through, for instance, home teaching, in which I strongly believe, or through informally offering friendship, assistance, or counsel. Reciprocally, I know that outside of my immediate family, my ward community cares more about me and my wife than does any other community in the world. Not that it is all sweetness and light: In every ward in which I have lived, there have been some members I did not like or respect very much, and there have been some bishops who seemed to me both pompous and ineffective. On the other hand, I'm pretty sure I rub people the wrong way as well. Yet, as Gene England insisted, that is precisely why "the Church is as true as the gospel." If we can't overcome ill feelings toward others, and learn to love all of God's children through our relationships in the Church, then for heaven's sake—where on earth *will* we learn to live the gospel of love?

So why do I stay in the Church? Why wouldn't I?

Note

1. Eugene England, "Why the Church Is as True as the Gospel," in England, *Why the Church Is as True as the Gospel* (Salt Lake City: Bookcraft, 1986), 1-15, originally published in *Sunstone*, Mar. 1986, 30-36.

Many people would agree that the "ward community cares more ... than does any other community in the world." Photograph taken in Buenos Aires by Marcos Brindicci for Reuters, February 2009.

© Corbis Images

One Woman's Spiritual Path

Grethe Peterson

Why I stay in the Church has a lot to do with how I was raised and what my spiritual path has been as an adult. My earliest memories include endless discussions about religion around the family dinner table. My parents raised questions, expected us to think critically, and often discussed their own conflicts around institutional loyalty and what we call free agency. Even though my parents were committed to the values of the Church and the sense of community it created ("a good way to raise a child"), I was aware of some of the tensions these questions created.

My parents stressed the importance of education and expected my brother and sisters and me to be well-informed, to be concerned about the well-being of others, and to work in the community, which often meant being good Democrats! All this took place in Utah County in the mid-twentieth century.

If I had not married Chase Peterson, my spiritual path might have been very different. We married in the temple, which was my commitment to begin the journey of building a testimony. Could I blend the values of my parents with the theology of the Church? I worked to come to my own understanding of the fundamental beliefs of the Church: The nature of God's presence in our lives. Christ's mission and ministry. Was Joseph a prophet? Was the Book of Mormon inspired of God? All these questions focused upon the centrality and goodness of the Church.

For a while I learned to ask fewer questions and become more involved, to appreciate the status quo more and criticize less. I became more open to the promptings of the Holy Spirit. I studied the scriptures and found strength from members of the wards in which we lived. Our early years were in New Haven, Connecticut, in a tiny branch that needed us. I was asked to teach Relief Society and, as is always the case, learned more than those whom I taught. I thrived on the preparation and presentation of those lessons.

Whether we were in branches or wards in Frankfurt, Germany; Cambridge, Massachusetts; or Salt Lake City, we associated with good people from varied backgrounds who were generous and loving in their callings. We were fortunate to have strong bishops who embraced my questions and encouraged me to serve.

There was one rather humorous and startling exception to someone tolerating our questions. In a Gospel Doctrine class soon after our first move to Salt Lake City in the sixties, the teacher took us aside after class and, as gently as he could, requested that we not ask questions during class because it interrupted his lesson plan. We smiled and agreed. For other reasons, we moved out of that ward. I have often wondered what we would have done if that kind of intolerance had been our permanent fare.

The fact is that my spiritual path has not always been clear or easy going. I have studied the gospel. I have been exposed to other faiths. I have been blessed with guides and teachers who have entertained my questions and given me confidence to keep moving and growing. These guides and teachers have come from a variety of settings. I have learned much from my husband and children. The women I've worked with in the Church have taught me about devotion and loyalty and strength of belief.

Many of my spiritual guides and teachers have been outside our Church. Without going into details, the wisdom and goodness of these women deeply touched my soul, changing me forever. Much of my growth has been the result of turning inward, of getting to know my soul and heart connections, separating ego from true belief. To know that God the Father, our Mother in Heaven, and our brother Jesus Christ are my mentors, and my strength, keeps me hopeful and moving forward. My life experiences have taught me the beauty and value of diversity. We may not look or think alike, but we are all God's children. We are all equal before our Lord, so our ability to reach out to one another brings us closer to heaven.

Have my spiritual awareness and broader education made me certain about the canon of the Church? Yes, in some ways, but not to the exclusion of finding truth in other faiths and philosophies. I have learned that there is a place for faith and there is a place for reason, but that utilizing both together keeps me in the right direction. I find the framework of the Church essentially right and regularly inspired. That is the context of my religious beliefs.

What have been the burning issues that have troubled me as I've traveled this spiritual path? For many years the issue of withholding the priesthood and temple blessings from worthy black members was extremely troubling to me. I could understand social and political challenges that confronted the Church in the nineteenth century, but I could not accept the ecclesiastical rationale many members gave. Our stake president in Cambridge knew of our concerns and supported us in our dissent on that issue. When Chase was made Dean of Admissions at Harvard College and the *Boston Globe* questioned whether, "since Dr. Peterson's Church does not admit black men to their priesthood," he would "admit black students to Harvard College," the issue grew even larger.

Given these concerns, June 9, 1978, was a remarkable day in our home in Cambridge. We made a lot of phone calls and heard from friends and colleagues all over the world. We thanked the Lord for this new revelation, acknowledging the inspiration and courage of President Kimball and the Council of the Twelve to seek a resolution.

The issue of women and the priesthood is still unresolved for me. I certainly understand, and have experienced, the many ways in which we women serve and grow from our service in the institutional Church. But it seems to me that the Church could benefit from the unity of male and female priesthood service on every level of leadership. I believe that through the power of prayer, as we engage in private deliberations with the Lord on this issue, the time may well come when the Lord feels that we are ready for this change, but probably not in my lifetime. I am okay with that.

The Church's position on homosexuality raises fundamental questions for me about how some define God's love and Christ's admonition "to love your neighbor as yourself." Sexuality is a private issue, but when sexual orientation results in citizens being discriminated against, something is wrong. With the question of gay marriage, this issue is taking on a more complicated dimension. But I return to Christ's model. He nourished the outcast and found ways to love all whom he met. Is it not possible for us to do the same? More importantly, can't I do the same?

My relationship with my Mother in Heaven is strong and constant, as well as sacred. For me, it is not a public issue. I accept and understand President Hinckley's request to pray to her only in private, and that is precisely what I have chosen to do.

So, this is my story. I believe there is a loving God and

Divine Mother who care deeply about their children. I believe that Christ is the son of God, who prepared the way for us. I believe that Joseph Smith was indeed a prophet who restored the gospel of Jesus Christ upon the earth at a critical time. The core beliefs of free agency, eternal progression, and continuous revelation are essential for my spiritual growth.

These are all reasons why I stay and have never thought of leaving. Through all of this, I hope I am a better person for having worked through the tenets of the Church on my own, just as my parents taught me to do, and for having acquired a personal testimony rather than having relied on someone else's word. I recommend it to young people today as a better course than asking them to obey blindly or follow the path of least resistance when conflicts arise.

Taking the Long View

Morris A. Thurston

In order to stay somewhere, one has to be there in the first place. I started out my life as a descendant of Mormon pioneers. My ancestors were not prophets or apostles or stake presidents or even bishops. They were just ordinary active Church members who served faithfully. They are not featured in history books, but they were the kind of sacrificing Saints who were critical to the growth of the Church.

My parents set sterling examples for my five sisters and me. We never doubted their love or their willingness to sacrifice for their family. They served the Church in local leadership positions and were always where they should be. Thanks in no small part to their encouragement, all of their children received college degrees and were married in the temple. Even though my parents have passed away, they have been an important reason for my staying. My upbringing in the Church instilled in me core values such as fidelity and constancy in marriage, love and familial respect, forbearance from harmful substances, and the importance of education and of service. I would need a very good reason to turn away from that.

I also stay because of my own life's experiences. I decided to go on a mission when I was nineteen. Being called to

Norway seemed like the perfect answer to a prayer. I would be returning to the birthplace of my paternal ancestors. However, my first Norwegian winter was like a dunk in icy water. I served in Trondheim, not far south of the Arctic Circle. The winter nights were long and the days short. The sun rose at about 10:00, never getting more than five degrees above the horizon, and by 2:30 it had disappeared.

Like most missionaries in those days, I arrived in the field knowing hardly a word of Norwegian. We were expected to absorb the language from senior companions who themselves spoke it poorly. Rejection was our common experience. The first Christmas, we asked our families at home to send toys for children at a state-run orphanage. We delivered them the day before Christmas and the children were thrilled, but the next morning the toys were back on the steps of our church because the orphanage would not accept charity from Mormons.

I am not easily intimidated or discouraged. Several of my friends and companions were sent home early, but I thrived. Even bad experiences became opportunities for growth, like the time I was sent to the police station to negotiate the release of an elder who had been jailed for public indecency. I had to negotiate with the authorities, using words that missionaries seldom had reason to use, and succeeded in freeing the elder only by promising that he would be on the first flight home.

In those days, I didn't openly challenge the accepted wisdom. One Sunday morning, quoting Joseph Fielding Smith, I contradicted a local member with five children who suggested that it was acceptable to use birth control for family planning. Another time I listened to two visiting missionaries from Scotland—a country where the baptismal rate had reached legendary proportions—talk about how we could use a "six-in-one" lesson plan to baptize tons of children. While

I was inwardly skeptical, I held my tongue. Now I know I shouldn't have.

I had questions that sometimes bothered me. It was difficult to warm to the concept that to have faith was to "hope for things which are not seen, which are true." To me, this definition was circular. It begged the question of what was true. In my experience, people could convince themselves to believe almost anything by fervently wanting it to be true. Surely there were honest members of other religions who had strong faith in their beliefs.

Nevertheless, I found inspiration in scriptures. I loved Ether 12:27, where the Lord explains that he gives us weaknesses so we will become humble and have faith in him and that he can turn our weaknesses into strengths. I decided I wouldn't worry about the fact that convert baptisms were as rare as a heat wave in Hammerfest. I would do my best, exercise faith, be open to inspiration, and let the Lord take care of the rest. It worked for me. My mission experience, therefore, is a reason I stay in the Church.

The decade following my mission was hectic, but I felt supremely confident that I could do anything with the Lord's help. My grades shot upward. I married the most beautiful girl I had ever met, who turned out to have a sparkling mind and a good heart, and with whom I am still in love forty-five years later. A top-tier law school education and a productive legal career followed.

As I matured and began to look at my religion with an inquisitive eye, however, I saw things that didn't seem right. The practice of denying the priesthood to African Americans was especially troublesome to me. Like many of my generation, I was dismayed by the reasoning behind the policy. Shortly after I returned from my mission, I heard a BYU Devotional talk given by Apostle Ezra Taft Benson denigrating the civil rights movement and implying that its leaders were communists or fellow travelers. I wrote a letter to the editor of the *Daily Universe* suggesting that if Elder Benson was going to speak on political issues, he should do so in a Forum meeting, not a Devotional. I worried about that for days, thinking I would become a pariah at BYU when it was published—but, of course, it never was.

Several years later, after reading Lester Bush's important *Dialogue* article, "Mormonism and the Negro Question," I felt even more strongly that the priesthood restriction was wrong. Why couldn't the brethren see that? I never doubted their good intentions but came to understand that they might be fallible human beings. Of course, I hadn't been called to lead the Church, but God had given me the right to think and seek personal revelation, and I saw that it was my responsibility to exercise that right in formulating my views on troublesome issues.

The Church presented many frustrations for me as the years flew by. I may just be a cynic by nature. If so, it is a trait that is difficult to fit into the umbrella of Mormonism's uncritical and cheerful approach. For example, I'm seldom inspired by testimony meetings. I feel trapped when I'm in the temple and wish the ceremony could be rewritten to eliminate redundancies. Although I appreciate the changes that have been made to eliminate anachronisms, I think more could be done. I dislike that we repeat the same lessons year after year in Sunday school, that teachers are instructed not to use materials outside the scriptures and general authority talks, and that truly thought-provoking questions are seldom posed.

And yet, when I take the long view, I see that many of the most sacred experiences in my life would not have happened had I let these irritations convince me to abandon my Church. I have time for only a couple of examples.

Our fifth child was named Elise. We had already lost one

baby, Lara, who was born prematurely and lived only ten days. Elise was a full-term, happy baby with sparkling eyes. One day when she was almost four months old, she suddenly died of SIDS—a crib death. It was the worst day of my life. We had just moved to Orange County a few months earlier, but we decided to bury Elise next to Lara at Forest Lawn in the Hollywood Hills. We didn't expect anyone from our current stake to make the two-hour round trip to the cemetery where we had planned a small graveside service. But when the time came, there was our stake president, our bishop, their wives, and other brothers and sisters from Orange County, as well as friends from our former ward in Glendale, letting us know they shared our grief. We've been fortunate in not needing the help of the Church often, but it is comforting and faith-promoting to know that members really do stand by you and offer true Christian service when needed.

I had the privilege recently of serving as a consultant to the legal series in the Joseph Smith Papers Project. I learned a lot about Joseph as I rubbed shoulders with other editors and scholars and researched original records from Joseph's lifetime. The Joseph Smith that emerged for me was not a perfect individual with perfect judgment, but I'm thankful my creed does not require that he be more than human. He was an extraordinary man whose occasional errors in judgment were overshadowed by his much greater positive contributions. This is another reason to stay.

Our present-day leaders also impress me. Those I know are honest and sincere. Unlike some Christian ministers who appear to be in the profession partly for the money, most LDS general authorities could earn more working in the occupations for which they were trained. It is remarkable to me how seldom they are tainted by scandal, something that cannot be said of the leaders of many other churches. I may not always share the views of our general authorities, but I realize they have given far more hours of service than I have and that they deserve to be listened to with respect.

When I received my patriarchal blessing as a teenager, I was told I had a special calling in the area of family history. During our first year of marriage, while we were attending BYU, Dawn and I became infused with a passion for discovering and telling the stories of our ancestors. Years later, while practicing law full time, I began researching the life of my Norwegian immigrant ancestor Tora Thurston. Over a ten-year period, I devoted countless nights, weekends, and holidays piecing together his life, and I was never happier than when I was immersed in the project. Finally I was able to publish a book-length biography of him and his family. Although he did not keep a diary or other intimate record, he was one of the faithful pioneers whose fascinating story needed to be told.

I received some critical acclaim for the book and was soon lecturing to groups on how to write a life story. About that time, Dawn pioneered a course in life-story writing at Santiago Canyon College. Before long, we were lecturing at BYU Education Week and other venues across the country about this meaningful aspect of people's lives. Eventually a how-to book Dawn and I wrote, *Breathe Life into Your Life Story,* was published. It was on an impulse from the Church that we were prompted to begin this quest to discover meaning in the lives of our ancestors; my conviction of the importance of it ties me to Mormonism and is another reason why I stay.

My interests also overlap with those of the Church in the field of ecclesiastical history. One of the most emotionally charged moments of my life took place in the Kirtland Temple a few years ago. We were there for a Sunday devotional meeting with other members of the Mormon History Association. The meeting was mostly musical, and Dawn and I were members of the choir. The temple has lofts in each of the four cor-

To stand in the Kirtland temple and imagine what transpired there can be emotionally and spiritually stimulating. Photograph by George Everard Kidder Smith, ca. 1935. © *Corbis Images*

ners, all of which our ad hoc choir filled to sing the hymns my
great-great-grandfather Edson Barney sang when he attended
the dedication of the temple in 1836. My heart has always
been especially touched by music. As we raised our voices in
song, I was suddenly struck with the image of how those early
members of the Church must have experienced that grand
day of spiritual outpouring when they sang

> The Spirit of God like a fire is burning;
> The latter day glory begins to come forth;
> The visions and blessings of old are returning;
> The angels are coming to visit the earth.
> We'll sing and we'll shout with the armies of heaven:
> Hosanna, hosanna to God and the Lamb!
> Let glory to them in the highest be given,
> Henceforth and forever: amen and amen!

My eyes filled with tears as I thought about the challenges those people were about to face but could not have
predicted—losing their savings in the Kirtland Safety Society
debacle, being driven out of Missouri, losing their prophet
to mob violence, and being asked to leave their homes in
Nauvoo for the wilderness of the West. I thought of how
many dropped out along the way and how my ancestors did
not, and I knew this was yet another reason why I remain.

Dawn and I may have married too young to have made
a rational decision about such a critical commitment. We
prayed and hoped the answer was inspired. We could not have
known how we would change over the next forty-five years—
how things would turn out, as they say. However, our belief
in an eternal partnership has brought us ever closer through
the waves of sadness, disappointment, and even occasional
disagreement that must be a part of every marriage. I am fortunate to be married to my best friend. I credit the Church

with providing an underpinning for the sense of eternal purpose that has cemented our bond.

The reasons I stay, therefore, are based to a large extent on my own personal narrative rather than on specific Church doctrines. It isn't that I reject the Book of Mormon or the Doctrine and Covenants. To the contrary, I believe both to be inspired and inspiring. I just can't get too worked up about specific doctrines when I see constant changes through the years. Sometimes the changes are explicit, sometimes implicit like the thinking regarding the Adam-God theory, blood atonement, and black people being less valiant in the pre-existence. These teachings simply fade away as though they had never existed, notwithstanding that prophets, seers, and revelators (for that is how we regard all apostles) have taught them in the past. I believe God is constant, but I also believe his will has been interpreted through men who were constrained by their own (and society's) pre-formed ideas. I believe this was true of prophets in Old Testament times, in New Testament times, and in our dispensation.

Church doctrine does provide a framework for understanding the purpose of life and what we can expect from the afterlife. But it is a loose framework. There is far more we don't know about the hereafter than we do know. To my way of thinking, the most important feature of LDS doctrine about "heaven" (the Celestial Kingdom, if you will) is that families will be together. How exactly will that work? Will our kids be with us or with their children? Will our grandchildren be with their maternal grandparents, their paternal grandparents, or their spouse's grandparents? If they have more than one spouse or more than one child, which family will they hang out with? Simple math tells you that within just a few generations, the possibilities become unfathomably complex. Mix in all of the people adopted into Joseph Smith's and other early Church leaders' families and it becomes even more confusing. So I don't worry too much about the here-after but rather adopt the attitude of Mickey Saxe's father in the movie, *Hannah and Her Sisters*. Mickey, played by Woody Allen, decides to become a Christian, agonizes over what will happen when he dies, and wonders why his Jewish father isn't stressed about it. His father replies: "Who knows what'll be? I'll either be unconscious, or I won't. If not, I'll deal with it then. I won't worry now."

So I will just try to live this life as honorably as I can, knowing that I will inevitably fall short of my own expectations, and let the next life take care of itself.

I have not been called to lead the Church and would never presume to preach my sometimes unorthodox ideas as doctrine. Nevertheless, there are things about the Church that make no sense to me. I think women are just as capable of receiving revelation as men and should be given an opportunity to serve in our presiding bodies. I think the Church should support those who decide to enter into a committed same-sex relationship. Believing in the value of marriage as we do, we should be on the side of those who are proponents of it. I believe the Church is too anxious to keep its priesthood control centralized and too quick to put down uncorrelated ideas at the expense of creativity. I would like to see the Church spend more resources on humanitarian service and less on proselytizing. I believe Church leaders should provide more financial information to Church members. Shouldn't those who contribute know how their contributions are being utilized?

I'm optimistic in thinking changes will occur in these areas, but I suspect they will happen slowly and in some cases probably not in my lifetime. In studying the past, however, I see favorable signs for the future. We are now told "we have nothing to do with polygamy," which is good—although we still perform polygamous eternal marriages. We now grant the priesthood to all worthy male members, which is a gratifying, though belated, change of direction. There are indications that the Church's official attitude toward our gay brothers and sisters is at least becoming less strident, though many members have a long way to go in this regard.

A couple of the brethren recently suggested that anti-immigration advocates in Utah should cool their rhetoric and treat our Hispanic brothers and sisters with more compassion. It is encouraging to see that there are some human rights issues where our leaders may be more progressive than many of the the members.

I'm encouraged when we're told the gospel encompasses all truths. I'm comforted that an apostle has said during my lifetime: "We are not so much concerned with whether your thoughts are orthodox or heterodox as we are that you shall have thoughts." Although such statements seem to have disappeared in the era of doctrinal correlation, I have faith that there will be other apostles who will express similar sentiments in the future.

Like the Reverend Martin Luther King, I have a dream. In my dream I am attending a general conference of the Church. I see twelve apostles sitting on the stand. My eyes slowly scan them from left to right. I know it is in the future because some of them are wearing colored shirts. Some have facial hair. Some are persons of color. Before my eyes reach the end of the row, I wake up. I'm not sure if there are any women on that row, but I hope there are. I can't tell if any of them is gay.

If the past is a guide, change comes as a result of people, both inside and outside the Church, raising issues that are seriously considered by our prophet and apostles, who then seek revelation to guide them. I stay, hoping that my voice and others can help prompt changes for the good, but all the while understanding my own limitations. I know that, like all fallible and imperfect humans, I could be mistaken. However,

I also know that it is my Christian responsibility to speak as honestly as I can and as humbly as I am able. I stay because I believe that doing so can make a difference.

My Reasons and Motivations

D. Jeff Burton

"Why do you stay?" That's a question I've heard many times over the course of the past twenty-five years. Like any difficult question, my answers have varied with (1) when the question was asked, (2) who was doing the asking, (3) why the question was asked, (4) what effect my answers might have on the listener, (5) the definition of "staying," and (6) how well I understood myself, my motivations, and my reasons.

For example, if we went back twenty-five years, my reasons would have included serving the needs of my wife, children, and parents; tradition and inertia; the expectations of neighbors, people in the ward, and friends; my callings for Church service; wanting authority and influence as a member of the bishopric; wanting to effect change; fear of the unknown; hope that the Joseph Smith story might be literally true; and especially for me, the sustaining excitement of the quarterly *Dialogue*, *Sunstone* magazine, and Francis L. Menlove's essays in both publications. However, in this piece I will explain where I am now as a member in the year 2011.

As for the "why" and "who is asking," I'm going to assume that readers are contemplating staying (or going) and will ponder my reasons or perhaps share them with others and are, therefore, of an open mind. If my grandkids were asking, or my bishop, I would be more circumspect and probably tailor my answers somewhat to their expectations or withhold an answer altogether. That potential vicissitude on my part is one of the issues I grapple with, as you will see.

As for the definition of staying, that has changed over the years for me. Early in my life, it meant toeing the line in every behavioral aspect of Mormonism. In recent years that need has relaxed and broadened. I am less active in Church meetings and probably considered by many of my Bountiful, Utah, neighbors to be on the borders of acceptability, but I still consider myself a stayer. I think this is an important definition that everyone must confront who finds himself in the same boat.

Identifying Reasons and Motives

For me, the most important aspect of this question is determining my real motives. In my thirties I found myself in psychoanalysis, which in those days everybody who could afford it did it. It was the Facebook of our day. For about a year, I met weekly with an analyst. After we dispensed with some Freudian foolishness, as Woody Allen has parodied so well in his movies, I had to learn how to recognize the reasons why I acted as I did or why I held certain attitudes about my family, business, or religion. It was an exciting time for me and well worth the effort. My analyst pushed me to examine myself week after week and constantly asked me, "Why did you do that?" "What else might have been driving you?" "What else?" "What was the motivation for that?" "Dig deeper!" After many months, I happened on motivations I had been unaware of. I did so through a self-evaluation technique that has served me well since, at least in moments when I can remember to use it.

Socrates left this aphorism: The unexamined life is not worth living. Everyone claims to agree with this, but it is my experience that people only think they have examined their lives and few really do. One nice guy in my ward told me, "I examined my life when I was twenty-six years old. For a week I prayed hard, thought about my life, and studied the scriptures. I found out what I needed to know about who I am. It was a good thing to do, but now I'm done with that phase of my life." Well, those are all good steps along the way, but to be effective, the examination should be continuous. It's not a static project that can be completed. Our behavior and the reasons for what we do change. I think the question of staying in or leaving the Church is of such importance that it should be revisited frequently.

During psychoanalysis, I learned that one uncovers multiple levels of motivation, given the effort. At first we quickly think of reasons we have been taught to think are acceptable, expected, and are easy to defend—the ones that make us sound impressive and upstanding. They are called "display motivations," and most of us rely on them, both implicitly and explicitly, to confirm or justify who we are and what we do in life. They are not the most important sources of attitudes or drivers of behavior. There are other deeper levels of explanations for what we do. These include the less-obvious, hidden motives that often elude us.

Let's take an example. Suppose someone is asked, "Why do you pay tithing?" The display reasons are usually that God has commanded us to do so, that it sets a good example for our kids, it is how God tests our faithfulness, because we love God, or because we couldn't afford to go without the blessings that accrue from paying tithing. These are acceptable responses that we often hear in sermons and read in Church publications. We say such things because they quickly come to mind and meet the criteria for uncontroversial discourse.

In most cases, we stop there and move on to the next question, especially at Church.

If we continue to look and dig down deeper, we find other reasons that still sound pretty good even if they are more self-serving. It takes effort to find these. It is also more difficult for other people to understand what we mean when we mention them. For tithing, to continue the same example, we might say we need to pay it in order to attend the temple, that we want to be accepted as part of the ward, that our spouses expect us to do it, and that it would be awkward to explain in front of the kids in tithing settlement at the end of the year if we didn't pay it.

But there is more. At the deepest level, perhaps hidden away from our conscious rationales, there are reasons we may not want to know about but are the real reasons for our actions even though they might be upsetting to ourselves and others. They require real introspection, thought, and enough time to tunnel down to find them. As it applies to tithing, the hidden motives might include being afraid of being punished by God and losing everything we have like Job, of losing the chance to attain a high Church position, of losing face, of wanting to be seen as a true believer, or of wanting to be seen as wealthy.

Which of these motivation levels is most important? All of them are relevant, depending on the priorities of the heart. But, most likely, the less obvious reasons are the strongest and the more visible explanations are dependent on the deeper ones. If that is in fact true, then unless we find and understand our subtle, more elusive desires, we cannot hope to manage them well. Finding and examining them requires hard work, personal honesty, and sometimes the help of others such as a loving spouse or a competent counselor. Once we have decided what influences our actions and attitudes, we can make better decisions about whether something is worth doing—if it is right for us and generally good.

To take Socrates one step further, the examined life can be worth living if we examine ourselves thoroughly, analyze what we find, and act wisely on the evidence.

Now to Get Personal

My current reasons and motives for staying in the Church look like the following, as far as I have been able to identify them:

My display reasons. I stay because people I admire and respect stay in the Church. I seem to have fallen into a unique calling to help those struggling to understand their place in Mormonism, and they themselves are trying to stay.[1] This alone sounds pretty good and might be sufficient reason for me to stay. Readers might be satisfied if I stopped here. In fact, I suppose I could expand endlessly on this one good reason and give examples of success and failure, peoples' stories, and why it is important, but if I did so, I wouldn't be completely open and honest with myself and others.

My less obvious reasons. It makes me feel good to help others. There are people who would be hurt if I went away. I feel a need to remain a part of the community. Mormonism is deeply embedded in my life and history. I'm a participating student of Mormonism, so I can't leave. I want others to see me as a Mormon follower of Jesus, a Mormon Christian.

My hidden motives. Now we go deeper. For instance, staying sometimes gives me the buzz of feeling like I might be in Fowler's Faith Stage 5, which is pretty far up there.[2] I like writing about my involvement in Mormonism and the attention and notoriety it provides me. I want people to like and admire me. I don't have anywhere else to go. I want to feel like I have some control over this problem. I feel some anger and frustration at the system. I want to change the Church. I feel some guilt at not having been completely open and honest in the past about my beliefs and this is my penance. I feel some fear in thinking about leaving the fold.

Now what? Now that I have identified several key reasons and motivations at each level, I need to analyze them and see where it leaves me if I act on them or not. My various motivations have generated the following questions:

Are my reasons and motives adequate? Yikes! Some of my motives for staying are disturbing. Many are self-satisfying and self-serving. Some are embarrassing, weak, or even dishonest. Plus, I worry that I'm still missing other potential motives. On the other hand, my motives aren't all bad. Some of them are idealistic and would seem to be sufficient reasons in themselves for staying.

Is staying good for my family? Staying or going won't affect my immediate family as much these days as it would have in the past. Most of my family now reside in the LDS borderlands. Those who don't are aware of where I'm coming from. Some of them think I've already gone, according to their more narrow definitions of staying. So this is not a big issue to me at this time.

If I stay, can I be honest with myself and others? I think that if I continue to stay, I can be mostly honest. Let's be candid and admit that it's a challenge in our current Church environment to be totally honest. I'm working on it, though, and I hope I can be more forthright.

Will staying have more of a positive or negative impact on other people? If I stay, it grants me some credibility with borderland people I'm trying to help. Going won't have any positive effects. Based on what I've heard from those who have responded to my column and book, I think staying will have more of a positive than negative effect.

Is it worth it to me to stay? I derive a lot of pleasure from what I do. So yes, it seems worth it. That is why I stay. I have a hopeful fantasy that sometime in the distant future, I might be able to write the following response to the question, "Why do you stay?"

My main motive is an overriding sense that Jesus is at the center of all we do, that Jesus is proud of us. I like the way we concentrate on learning to live Jesus's teachings. I really feel this is Jesus's work.

I appreciate the way the Church champions the goals of peace, rejection of war, justice for everyone, and equality of women and men. I have the wonderful feeling that everyone is accepted just as they are. I appreciate the way the system relies on all of us and trusts us.

At a friend's temple wedding, the overwhelming sense of hope and love that all of us—members and non-members alike—felt in the sealing room was unforgettable.

Every Sunday morning I wake up with excited feelings of anticipation as I get ready to go to Church. Time stops when I'm there and I wish we could stay longer! After Church I leave with feelings of great personal worth, as if I have been re-energized for living Jesus's teachings about honesty, kindness, caring, and patience. I really love our Church services and appreciate the interesting gospel study we have.

When we study the gospel, I feel that the lessons are balanced and that there are no hidden agendas. The lessons are always fresh and pertinent to my life. The authors of the lessons are clearly identified. We are encouraged to respond with comments, questions, and suggestions. All sides of every historical event or issue are explored. I really love the openness and honesty of it all. I know I can say anything in class and not be judged.

I'm thrilled by our ward's efforts to lift up the poor, the widowed, and the sick and the service we render to those less fortunate. I am honored to be able to support our various outreach programs such as our humanitarian aid that provides education and health services to less fortunate people around the world.

At Church and in Church publications, I'm never made to feel guilty or fearful, only compassion and love for my fellow beings. I never feel like I'm being coerced to obey orders—the emphasis is always on understanding and choosing what I'm comfortable with. No one is controlling me. We are encouraged to be curious and creative. I feel we are learning to move to Fowler's Stage 5 as we are able to, and helping one another get there. That seems to be our destination.

I sense in our leaders a great deal of humility and love. They definitely are in Fowler's Stage 6. I like the openness and frankness with which they deal with controversies. All of their minutes, for example, are open for us to review. It is heartening to know that our leaders trust us enough to share all the relevant information they have with us, including the results of their deliberations, and that they consider our input into important policy decisions. There is the sense that everyone is entitled to inspiration to help guide the Church.

I don't think of it as staying with "the" church. I think of it as staying with "my" Church and "our" Church. I have such a feeling of belonging and being cherished. Why wouldn't I stay?

Notes

1. I have written *For Those Who Wonder: Managing Religious Questions and Doubts* (Bountiful, UT: IVE, 1985) and write a regular column, "Braving the Borderlands," in *Sunstone* magazine, both of which address concerns people have when questioning whether they should stay in the Church.

2. James W. Fowler, *Stages of Faith: The Psychology of Human*

Development (New York: HarperOne, 1995). Fowler has suggested, and mostly substantiated, that religious adults reside in, or move through, six faith stages. Stage 1: demonstrates a rigid, authoritarian, fear-based personal religion, with no allowance for error. Stage 2: considers blessings to be based on obedience, misfortunes on sin; assumes the world is mostly black and white and follows a formula for living. Stage 3: accepts religious teachings, scriptures, and claims without much question; learns and follows expectations of his or her religious group. Stage 4: shows curiosity, skepticism, individualism, and accepts diversity and paradox; dismisses group expectations as not as important as individual convictions. Stages 5 and 6: shows a commitment to general and universal justice, truth, and honesty; considers authority to rest within self; makes faith universally applicable; practices selfless devotion to others; achieves high levels of personal honesty, integrity, and fairness.

Despite Some Troublesome Topics,
I Am a Mormon to My Bones

J. Frederick "Toby" Pingree

I have deep Mormon roots. I am a third-generation Latter-day Saint on one side of my genealogical tree and a fifth-generation on the other. My early years did not portend a particularly challenging relationship with the Church. I grew up in Salt Lake City. The prophet of my youth was Heber J. Grant and he lived in my ward. My high-school seminary and college Institute of Religion classes were taught by some of the most able and enlightened teachers the Church has ever produced—men like Lowell Bennion and Marion D. Hanks. My life followed the orthodox trajectory. I was an Eagle Scout and a Master M-Man.[1] I served a full-time mission and married in the temple. As one friend said, only half jokingly, "Toby, you were punched out and assembled at a Mormon factory."

Yet despite my conformist, establishment background, I have struggled with certain aspects of the faith I inherited from my fathers. Three issues in particular have been and continue to be troublesome to my faith.

1. The unequal treatment of God's children within the Church.

The concept that God loves all his children has great appeal to me, as well as significant scriptural support. "All are alike unto God, black and white, bond and free, male and female," writes Nephi (2 Ne. 26:33), and Paul told the Galatians that "there is neither Jew nor Greek, there is neither bond nor free, there is neither male nor female: for ye are all one in Christ Jesus" (Gal. 3:28).

In the practices of what we call the Restored Church, some of God's children have been and currently are treated less equally than others. Women are denied participation in the Church's governing bodies, cannot hold the priesthood, and study materials and lessons dictated and controlled by the men. Non-white Church members, mostly from Third World countries, comprise approximately half the Church membership worldwide, yet only a small fraction of general authorities come from this group and no person of color has ever been called into the highest echelon of Church leadership.

For more than a century, persons of black African descent were not given the priesthood nor admitted to temples, thereby, according to the then prevailing Mormon doctrine and practice, relegated to a secondary status in this life and the next. While we now celebrate the reversal of this segregationist practice, vestiges of its racist implications persist today in unofficial writings and publications sold through Church-related outlets and in the attitudes and behaviors of some Latter-day Saints.

2. The retention of polygamy as a doctrine.

Three of my great-grandfathers and one grandfather were polygamists. Among them, they had a total of seventeen wives. In family circles, the commitment and devotion these

76

[Handwritten margin annotations:]

Top margin: Women are in governing bodies and always have been after R.S. established.

Left margin: ① This has changed. Gong, Soares ② Women share in priesthood Power and exercise it in the temple and in their other callings + home responsibilities.

Right margin: No g cultural practise is not doctrine,

Bottom margin: Through temple ordinances we hold the priesthood with husbands. I'm without husbands.

Saints demonstrated in living "the principle" is still considered heroic. To this day, I have great admiration and respect for all those who diligently practiced plural marriage. But as an eternal principle, it does not make sense to me—neither common sense nor theological sense.

If this form of marriage is necessary *no* to attain the highest state of exaltation in the next life, as was taught by nineteenth-century Mormon leaders, it seems that a disproportionate number of women will be going to heaven and that few males will be able to qualify before the available women are spoken for. In other words, it implies that men are less worthy or righteous than women. By contrast, we are told, and it is my conviction, that the loftiest relationship that can exist in this world is between two loving spouses—not an unequal number of women tied to one man—who are united in their commitment to one another's happiness.

While the contemporary Church goes to great lengths to distance itself from the practice of polygamy and assures the world that there is no such thing as modern Mormon polygamy, our leaders have yet to renounce plural marriage as a doctrine. In fact, eternal polygamous marriages are performed routinely in our temples.

3. Repression of independent thought and individual study.

In earlier times, it seemed that Church members were encouraged to seek knowledge and truth wherever they could be found. They were told to "study and learn, and become acquainted with all good books and with languages, tongues, and people" (D&C 90:15). If an important subject needed to be taught and talent was not available in the community, teachers were brought in from the outside.[2]

Differences in belief among early Church leaders were

well-known, and serious gospel students had to study issues themselves and reflect on them spiritually to determine which were applicable in their lives. Errors in doctrine were tolerated, if expressed in good faith. Joseph Smith wanted the liberty of being able to think for himself, and he extended this privilege to his followers.[3] In 1969 a member of the Church's First Presidency, Hugh B. Brown, reaffirmed the principle in a talk at Brigham Young University when he said, "Preserve, then, the freedom of your mind in education and in religion, and be unafraid to express your thoughts and to insist upon your right to examine every proposition."[4]

We now live in an era of supervised learning in the Church where acceptable teaching materials are nearly identical from year to year and are simplified so that little real information is presented. Predominantly they reference remarks by Church leaders and scriptural passages that are carefully chosen to be sure that they espouse approved doctrines.

The Church's education establishment carefully culls those who apply to teach within its institutions and accepts only people who will teach the current orthodoxy. Only historians whose orientation is toward faith-promoting history are considered acceptable. Group study and discussion outside official venues are discouraged and sometimes prohibited. Few men who hold positions of authority consider the likelihood that where there is an open, balanced discussion of Mormon issues in an independent forum, the results will be salutary.

In summary, these are the main sources of intellectual and spiritual irritation to me within the Church. Why do I continue to be an active, faithful Latter-day Saint in paying my tithing, sorting clothes at Welfare Square, attending weekly services, performing monthly temple rites, completing my assignment to visit people in our ward, and helping to clean the chapel? There are a number of reasons, but the following four are primary:

writers opinions only

- I believe that Joseph Smith was a unique American visionary who qualified to be able to speak to and for God. My view of him has changed in many ways since I first began thinking seriously about the founder, but still I adhere to the position that, by the gift and power of God, he was the agent in producing the Book of Mormon, whatever its origins. My beliefs evolved from a foundation of sand to one of bedrock during my early months as a young missionary. Sick with dysentery and jaundice, I nevertheless explored the simple truths of the gospel with the people of Guatemala and had several convincing personal spiritual experiences confirming to me that I was on the Lord's errand.

- I am continually sustained by the basic conviction that there is a God in heaven who is literally my father. I believe God loves me unconditionally and sent his son to die for me. Christ suffers with me through earthly trials and comprehends my circumstances because of his mortal experiences. I don't understand why and how he accomplishes this, but I am confident that someday I will understand it.

- I am a Mormon to my bones. My ties to the Restored Church must be intertwined with my DNA. I am buoyed up whenever I gather with the Saints, be it when I am meeting with a priesthood group in the Andes or attending a discussion group at the Sunstone symposium—all places where I learn from others and am listened to respectfully. The Church provides me the opportunity to serve and to be served. I bear the controlling and sometimes repressive aspects of the Church as burdens because I suspect those who run the institution are doing the best they can. In return, I can help by staying involved, partaking of the light of others, and letting my light be seen to the degree that it is requested.

- I am comforted by Mormonism's promises that the ties

that matter most on earth will continue when we move to another sphere of existence. Commitments made in the temple assure me that the long love affair I have had with my wife, Phyllis, will continue beyond time and that I will somehow also be involved with other members of my family in the eternities. I believe that my endearing friendships with others will also be part of my eternal fulfillment.

My experience as a faithful but questioning Latter-day Saint is not all that uncommon, I suspect. My struggle with balancing faith and reason does not erode my commitment to or involvement in the Church. I stay active and serve when called, hopefully learning lessons along the way. I try to be an influence for good and to take advantage of opportunities when they present themselves, striving in my own way to make the Church a better and more inviting place for everyone.

Notes

1. "M-Men" stood for males who were involved in a Mutual Improvement Association program for young adults, eighteen to thirty years of age, wherein female participants were called "Gleaners," inspired by the biblical character Ruth. The young people were commissioned to complete various tasks in four categories (spiritual, cultural or athletic, creative, and executive) in order to receive the title of *Master M-Man* for men and *Golden Gleaner* for women. On completion of the tasks, they were given a lapel pin to wear to Church activities. The MIA sponsored elaborate dances for these young adults that were called Gold and Green Balls. See Ardis Parshall, "Master M-Men and Golden Gleaners," online at *Keepapitchinin*, www.keepapitchinin.org.

2. An example was Joshua Seixas, who taught Joseph Smith and others Hebrew in the Kirtland-era School of the Prophets.

3. B. H. Roberts, ed., *History of the Church of Jesus Christ of Latter-day Saints,* 7 vols., 2d ed. rev. (Salt Lake City: Deseret Book, 1950), 5:340.

4. Hugh B. Brown, "An Eternal Quest: Freedom of the Mind," a speech delivered at Brigham Young University, May 13, 1969, in BYU's *Speeches of the Year,* 1969.

A Coin Balanced on Its Rim

Lavina Fielding Anderson

Recently I received an email from my niece, Shalom, who was a child when I was excommunicated from the LDS Church in 1993. She wanted to know what had happened and why I still attend Sunday services. Her question gave me an opportunity to reflect on my life during the intervening time. Just prior to having heard the heavy news fifteen years ago, I was standing in a meadow up to my waist in dozens of shades of green. As I stood there, three understandings came to me with unmistakable clarity and authority: first, that I was going to be excommunicated; second, that I was not to go to the court convened to give me that verdict; and third, that it would be a long time before I was reinstated. The first two happened. On the third, I'm still counting.[1]

Because opportunities for bearing testimony are quite rare for me these days, I'd like to use this occasion to do so now despite my somewhat ambivalent status of being *of* but not *in* the Church. We tend to see people as either in or out, like flipping a coin: tails you're in, and heads you're out. I see myself as occupying the more ambiguous position of a coin that is balanced on its rim.

I want to make it crystal clear that I am speaking only for myself, and I want absolutely nothing I say to be interpreted as criticism of anyone else's choices, whether that choice is to stop thinking about a troubling Mormon question and continue to participate with peace of mind, to drift quietly into inactivity, to seek spiritual experiences in a different tradition or faith community, to say "that's the last straw" and slam the door as you walk out, or to look a leader squarely in the eye and say: "This is what I believe. This is what I don't believe. Do what you have to do." I respect, accept, and admire all of those choices. They all represent sincere acts of faith and demonstrate real integrity. I'm not advocating my solution for anyone. I am also not accepting anyone else's criticism or judgment of my situation. What I have chosen is right for me.

In spite of being excommunicated, there are six reasons why I keep going to ward meetings week after week, month after month, year after year. The first is for my family. The gospel was everything to my parents, their source of meaning, order, hope, and help. They both served missions in the 1930s. They struggled financially but were always faithful. My father served as bishop in two wards during a time when local members not only contributed most of the money but most of the labor to build their own chapels. Following our parents' example, all six of us children had callings in the Church. All of us served missions, and all married in the temple.

My mother's family, who were from Tennessee, joined the Latter-day Saints in Nauvoo. My father's family joined in England and immigrated to Utah in 1857. I'm proud of that heritage and one reason I kept going is that I wanted our son Christian to be proud of it. It meant something to me, and I wanted it to mean something to him. I wanted him to know that, even though the Church severed its ties with me, I refused to sever my ties with those generations that came before me. Christian has continued our family tradition by

A temple can be a place of peaceful retreat or an impenetrable castle.
Photograph by Walter Bibikow, La Jolla, California. © *Corbis Images*

serving a mission and marrying in the temple. Because of our family's Mormon heritage, those were shared experiences that brought us closer together. Because of my status, I sat in the overcrowded, overheated lobby of the San Diego temple while Christian was being married inside, but Lorie Winder Stromberg sat outside with me, an act of friendship that I'll always cherish.

The second reason I stay connected to the Church is that Paul and I met, courted, married, and have lived as Mormons. I didn't want my relationship with the Church to come between us and our marriage. Our temple sealing and the covenants we made at marriage are significant to us. Paul wanted a Mormon wife, and I felt that he deserved one, just as I wanted and felt I deserved a Mormon husband. During the two years that I was growing more concerned about the problem of ecclesiastical abuse in the Church, Paul played devil's advocate. He is the fairest person I know. He will bend over backward to see another person's point of view, whereas I am much more inclined to impose my point of view. Never once during that time did he try to tell me what to do. He always wanted to discuss all the information available, talk about it, and see it from every angle, then work through the consequences together. I absolutely cannot say enough good about him.

When the letter was delivered scheduling my disciplinary council, there were no more questions from Paul. Nor did he say "I told you so." We still share a common perspective and think the same Mormon things are inspirational or funny and outrageous. Quite frequently, after something particularly dumb has happened (the Mitt Romney campaign supplied a fairly steady supply for awhile), Paul will shake his head and say, "What a strange Church you used to belong to, Lavina."

The third reason I stay is that I love Mormonism. I was moved by the Book of Mormon and gained a testimony of it before I knew what to think about Joseph Smith. The Book of Mormon has continued to speak to me as scripture. When President Benson began urging people to read the Book of Mormon every year, I thought that was a good idea and have done it, either on paper or by listening to audio tapes, every year since. I love Joseph Smith. I don't always *like* Joseph Smith, and I'm pretty sure he got some important things wrong, but I love his spiritual and intellectual aliveness, his willingness to listen and think about things in a new way.

Fourth, I love Mormon theology. I love its emphasis on grace *and* works. I love its open canon of scripture. I love the presence of a Mother in Heaven even though we aren't supposed to talk about her at present. I love the doctrine of free agency and the doctrine of eternal progression even though the first has been dumbed down to "moral agency" and the second, based on President Lorenzo Snow's pithy epigram, "As man is, God once was, and as God is, man may become," was damped down during President Hinckley's administration to "a little couplet that we don't know too much about."

Fifth, I love the Mormon community. Paul and I have lived in the same ward for thirty-one years now, so we're some of the older people in our congregation. Pieces of it have the comfort of familiarity—like which bench we sit on, the fact that the air conditioning has frost forming on the windows of the Relief Society room, that we can count on the Primary kids to sing for special programs with enthusiasm if not tunefulness, and that the bishop will wear a funny tie at least a couple of times a month.

Parts of it aren't always comfortable. I am not happy with the fact that sacrament speakers, including visiting high counselors, are now asked to base their talks on a general conference talk from the *Ensign* magazine. Usually Paul sits on the aisle so he can take the sacrament and then indicate to the deacon to go on so that I don't have to personally refuse it. A few weeks ago when I was sitting on the aisle, an elderly high priest made a big deal of stretching way past me to hand the tray of bread to Paul. Maybe he was just being tactful. Maybe he thought I'd contaminate the tray if I touched it. But when he came around with the water, I grabbed it from him, glared, and passed it to Paul, then back to him. Then I got the giggles.

As this illustrates, I still find occasion to laugh about situations I find myself in. I also smile about situations the Church gets itself into. I was waiting to see what President Monson's first official letter would address, and it provided me with a double whammy of amusing trivia. First, he asked that there be no visual aids in sacrament meeting. Second, speakers were to stop asking the congregation to look up scriptures or to follow along as they are read. This was the extent of the advice in his first communication, but immediately it made me think of a really unforgettable talk in our ward in which the speaker demonstrated several methods of eating Oreos, including dipping them in milk. I can't remember what the point of his talk was. On the other hand, the member of the bishopric who read President Monson's letter was sufficiently puzzled that he felt the need to come up with a defense: "I guess that will cut down on the ruckus during sacrament meeting." A couple of weeks later when several young women were reporting their camp experience, one of the girls pulled out her scriptures and said, "My favorite scripture is Proverbs—" then quickly interrupted herself to exclaim, "Don't look it up!" Paul and I both got the giggles.

Emily Dickinson said she saw the world "New Englandly." I see the world Mormonly. It may be the most important part of my identity. These are my people, my music, my mode of prayer, my history, my family. The steps I took to put my membership in jeopardy, I did deliberatively and because I genuinely could not imagine acting differently. Even though

I did not feel called to correct the Church (that is Jesus's job, not mine), I did feel called to be a witness in the household of faith about things that had gone awry in that household. I sincerely had the hope of nudging the Church back to its better self on how victims of child abuse, for instance, were being unintentionally treated as transgressors while the transgressors were being protected for the sake of Church image. I saw the exclusion and abuse of Church scholars, feminists, and homosexuals for the sake of institutional purity as dreadful violations of gospel principles and as self-inflicted wounds for which the Church would suffer greatly—as indeed it has. Standing up was an act of conscience, of love, of faith. I would not have left the Church on my own, so even though the Church tore up my membership, that was not a reason to leave, as I saw it. Although I am no longer a Church member, I *am* still a Mormon. I want to be in the right place when the time comes for our paths to rejoin.

It has not been easy following this path, although it has not been as hard as I thought it might be. My own sloth and boredom ("*Not* another high council talk on following the prophet!") are much greater obstacles than theological differences or being offended by insensitive members or feeling that it's just not worth being where I am not wanted. The Church had power over my membership but does not have power over my Mormonness, which I continue to claim as my own destiny.

I can see now that before I was excommunicated I received powerful spiritual preparation for the potential consequences of my behavior. Even though part of me did not really believe that the Church would discipline someone for telling the truth, I knew that loyalty, conformity, and obedience were highly regarded values that I was transgressing by speaking out. I felt (and still do) that I was acting out of love, loyalty, and commitment. My patriarchal blessing cautions me more than once to be humble, so I monitored myself to be sure I was not acting out of pride, hostility, or indifference to my leaders in the months between publication of the *Dialogue* article and conversations with my stake president. I truly and sincerely feel that I was none of these, so I did not feel that the rejection of my message had much power over me.

I have talked before about what draws me to Mormonism —what I love about my religious tradition—but I need to say that the sixth most crucial reason for me to stay in the Church is that I not only love the Church, but in some ways it loves me back. I *feel* loved within the Church—not by the stake president and various officials, particularly, but by my Heavenly Father and Heavenly Mother and truly by Jesus. I can't help loving them in return. I want to love them more deeply, in part by keeping the promises I made at baptism and in the temple. Those promises are important to me. Do I think someone can make promises in an other-than-Mormon context and keep them with the same fidelity and be cherished in the same way by God? Absolutely. But this is the mode—the Mormon mode—in which I choose to keep my promises. I don't think a few words in a temple made my sealing to Paul any more real, but I think our shared commitment to live accordingly *does* make it real. I think God honors many kinds of promises made in many places, and what we said in the temple is one example of the kind of thing I think God acknowledges.

Lest I come across as too ghastly noble, I have to admit that I'm stubborn. Sometimes I feel that if I left, "they" would win. By being there every Sunday, I'm claiming a place and saying, "Deal with it." I'm saying, "I'm not going anywhere. Get over it."

Last week I was looking at the meadow with all its varieties of green and thinking about what happened fifteen years before. I realized that if I could do it all again, I would change nothing. We live so much of our lives in compromise and half-measures, in *almosts* and *not quites,* that it's a privilege to take a clear stand on an issue of conscience. As I review those fifteen years, I realize I have lived through plenty of moments of pride and sloth and selfishness, but I believe I have also lived with dignity, integrity, and a good sense of humor. After fifteen years, I have a sense of peace and feel a greater sense of reciprocal love from my family, from good friends, and above all from the Savior, who said, "Inasmuch as ye have done it unto one of the least of these ... ye have done it unto me" (Matt. 25:40).

Note

1. In the spring 1993 issue of *Dialogue,* I published a chronological list of 133 instances of what I saw as the Church's growing hostility toward historians. The stake president had a copy of this article when he called me in for the first interview and told me I needed to apologize for the article and stop talking to people who were having difficulties with the Church. I spent the summer, as usual, at our cabin in the mountains above Salt Lake City and communicated with the stake president by mail. At stake conference in September where Paul, Christian, and I sang in the choir, the stake president greeted me cordially. Fifteen minutes after we reached home, his counselor delivered a letter summoning me to a high council court. As a result of that court, which I did not attend, the stake president excommunicated me. The original grounds cited were for "conduct unbecoming a member," but the excommunication itself was for "apostasy." No instructions were included about attaining readmittance. When I inquired, the stake president responded: "You must put away any items or conduct that makes [sic] you feel that the 'Lord's anointed' are wrong or unrighteous." When I pointed out that I had never taken that position—quite the con-

trary, in fact—and that it had never been one of the issues we had discussed, he did not answer. He never has, nor have either of his two successors in that office.

I Trust the Data

Gregory A. Prince

The conversion of George Prince in South Africa in 1855 marked the first of five generations of Princes preceding me in this Church. That is not the reason I stay. A religion that does not work for us now has little staying power, regardless of how well it may have worked for our ancestors. But in fact, Mormonism works for me, just like it did for my forebears. So I stay.

Having spent thirty-five years of my life as a biological scientist, I bring a scientific perspective to the question. Several years ago I interviewed Nobel laureate Paul Boyer, who pointed out that of all the natural sciences, biology was the least conducive to religious activity. To reinforce his point, he cited surveys at the beginning and end of the twentieth century that confirmed this finding. He said I was at high risk of becoming an atheist, which is what he had become. In fact, he said he thought of proselytizing me because he thought I showed promise. As a molecular biologist and the only Mormon ever to win a Nobel Prize—yes, there has been one, although you didn't read about it in the *Church News*—Dr. Boyer had abandoned his faith decades earlier.

Somehow I avoided that fate, never experiencing the crisis of faith he predicted even though I was completely immersed in experimental biology, perhaps the riskiest challenge to belief within the already high-risk field of biology. Rather than taking me away from faith, biology gave me tools with which to examine the Church and ultimately embrace it in a way I never could have imagined. The tools of scientific methodology, which transformed the western world, have utility beyond the boundaries of science. In fact, they have been appropriated, usually without attribution, by virtually every academic discipline. Witness the title of one academic periodical: *The Journal for the Scientific Study of Religion*.

In examining my own faith, I found that science was useful in looking at some questions but not at others and that it was not difficult for me to distinguish between the two categories. For instance, the declaration "God lives" falls outside the scope of scientific inquiry, but the nature of revelation may be examined scientifically. Similarly, the declaration that "Joseph Smith was God's prophet" is an expression of faith, but the manner in which he functioned as a prophet is accessible to scientific inquiry. As a result, I can summarize my encounter with Mormonism in four words: "Go with the data." If a question is susceptible to examination, I want to make sure for myself that the data are solid. Then I go with the facts. If it is something that cannot be measured and tested, I am willing to accept it as a matter of faith and be content with it. This approach has not failed me. I have never walled off an inconvenient truth with a "Do Not Enter" sign, and I can say with some confidence that I don't believe I ever will. I feel sorry for people who, from my perspective, run from hard questions because they are afraid of what they may find.

I have immersed myself in collecting data relating to Mormonism for over two decades, first in conducting an eight-year study of the LDS priesthood that involved reading hundreds of thousands of pages of manuscripts and publications, some of which pre-dated the founding of the Church in

1830. Next I undertook a ten-year study of Church President David O. McKay, beginning with his 40,000-page diary and extending to hundreds of thousands of pages of other materials, along with 200 interviews, including interviews with two Church presidents. Finally, I am conducting an ongoing study of Leonard Arrington, the former Church Historian, who was one of the giants of Mormon historiography.

Nobody can claim to have seen it all, but I have seen plenty—enough that I doubt there are significant surprises out there that I have not been alerted to. Let me share just a few of the foundations of my faith in light of the consideration I have given to the data I have collected on Church topics. My observations will not be directly related to the data, but they indicate my overall sense of things at this point in my life as someone who remains engaged in the Church. I am in my seventh decade of life, so perhaps some of my observations contain hints of wisdom. You will be the judge of that.

1. I detect the presence of God within Mormonism.

That is a statement of faith and not of data. I see his hand and work frequently, sometimes on a macro scale but more often in the lives of ordinary people who live in near-anonymity and do good works. There was a time—and some of you will understand that certitude peaks at about nineteen years of age—when I thought God was only within Mormonism. I have subsequently witnessed too much of him in other Churches and elsewhere to deny that his presence is everywhere, and I have come to realize that it is not up to me to tell God where he can spend his time.

2. Doubt is essential to a healthy faith.

When life progresses in an orderly fashion, with the righteous prospering and the wicked suffering, faith is easy and perhaps not necessary. But when life does not follow that formula, doubts arise naturally and we should not be ashamed of them. Instead, we should look at them as doorways that lead to increased faith. In 1955 when I was seven years old, the world of amusement changed forever with the opening of Disneyland. I grew up in Los Angeles, and within months our family took the one-hour drive to the exciting new theme park. One of the attractions, taken from the classic children's book, *The Wind in the Willows,* was "Mr. Toad's Wild Ride." We sat in the little car on a twisting, turning ride through the English countryside of a century ago. Along the way we saw road signs, among which were Derbyshire (pronounced Derbysure), Devonshire (pronounced Devonsure), and one I had never heard of but have since visited frequently: Not-so-shire. Healthy doubt leads to healthy faith. When I place my religion under a microscope and examine the possibility that it might not be true, I begin to own my faith rather than to borrow it.

3. Humankind can progress without limits.

No theology could be more optimistic than one that proclaims humankind's infinite potential. The best reward for a well-lived life is eternal progression, not eternal bliss. Mormon theology is the American dream writ large. It is also a call to action in the here-and-now, for we will take with us the tools that we have acquired and sharpened during this life and continue to use and improve them in the next.

4. On a good day, Joseph Smith was brilliant.

Today's Church leaders, at all levels, have good days and they also have bad days. It was the same for Joseph Smith.

I understand this. In my own career, I have had a few very good days and a lot of bad ones. One person I interviewed told me Church President Harold B. Lee asked him about his brother who had left the Church. When the man replied that his brother had left because he worked with the general authorities and saw the workings of power up close, President Lee replied, "I can think of much better reasons to leave the Church. Doesn't he realize that we are just human beings trying to do our best?" When I see Church leaders doing their best, it is a beautiful thing. At other times, I rejoice that we share so much in common.

5. We are all flawed and need each other's help.

We are physicians, trying to heal each other within our community of believers. Even as a physician without patients is not complete, we are not complete outside a community of other believers. Mormonism is empty if it is practiced in isolation. The inner religious life is essential, but without an outer religious life in a community of believers, it is the sound of one hand clapping.

6. Revelation flows up.

"Trickle-up" revelation is arguably the most important force of revelation shaping the day-to-day Church in which we live. If you doubt that statement, consider the Relief Society, Mutual Improvement, Sunday School, Primary, Welfare, Genealogy (Family History), and Young Adult Programs all began as grass-roots initiatives on the part of creative Church members and were then embraced by the central Church. This means that phrases such as "magnifying one's calling," "men should be anxiously engaged in a good cause, and do many things of their own free will, and bring to pass much righteousness," and "be not weary in well-doing, for ye are laying the foundation of a great work. And out of small things proceedeth that which is great," are not platitudes but a real call to action. I have been a first-hand witness of and participant in the birth of the Young Adult program in Southern California in the early 1970s and a first-hand witness of the effect of Lester Bush's landmark monograph on blacks and the priesthood in the mid-1970s. A Church that not only allows but expects its members to assist in its continual transformation by placing their unique gifts at the altar has my vote.

7. The missionary program holds the Church together.

My experiences as a missionary in Brazil over forty years ago shaped my life and continue to inform it. If the collective efforts of 60,000 missionaries did not result in a single baptism, the missionaries and the Church would yet be better off for them having served. Our oldest son recently completed service in the California San Bernardino Mission, and his weekly letters bore witness to the transformational power of a mission and took me back to my own experiences long ago and far away.

8. Families really do come first.

Mormons did not invent the family, but we have taken the concept to another level. The doctrine surrounding the eternity of the family bond is beautiful and pure even if its details are as yet unanswered. (Where *will* we spend Thanksgiving in the next life?) Nor is Mormonism's contribution limited to the then-and-there. One need only look at the patronage of our Family History Centers by non-Mormons to know that no other institution has done as much to help people discover their forbears. Perhaps this is one of the most important gifts of Mormonism to the world.

9. The Church is the village that helps us raise our children safely.

It's a hazardous world, particularly for children. They need all the help they can get. I am well aware of the Church's deficiencies when it comes to the youth, perhaps the most irritating of which is the fact that, as the kids say, Church is boring. There is much that can be done to improve the youth programs, and perhaps a call to action will motivate us to put on our creative-thinking caps. Even with these deficiencies, the Church is nevertheless a strong beacon of light in the midst of a storm. One of the most gratifying things in my life has been to hear my children later express their appreciation for the standards they once considered restrictive but now realize are a foundation upon which they can build their entire lives. Seeing so many of their peers come undone at an early age helps to reinforce this lesson.

10. We have the potential to be a major player on the international stage.

Individual Mormons have risen to prominence in many fields, but as an institution we remain well short of our potential. We need to sit down at the same table as our neighbors and learn to speak their language. We need to acknowledge that they have much to offer and that we can all learn from each other. This is what President Monson meant when he said, at his first press conference on February 4, 2008,

> I think we should not be sequestered in a little cage. I
> think we have a responsibility to be active in the commu-

nities where we live—all Latter-day Saints—and to work cooperatively with other churches and other organizations. My objective there is that I think it is important that we eliminate the weakness of one standing alone, and substitute for it the strength of people working together. There are many efforts where, as we get together as various religions in the community and work toward the common goal, it shall be successful. We have cooperated with Red Cross, the Catholic Church and other churches, to make this a better community and a better world. I believe in that spirit.

There are authentically bad people in the world, and it will take a combined effort on the part of others to prevail against them. The last thing we need is to quarrel with our Christian neighbors or with people of other faiths or good people who have agnostic or atheistic leanings. By joining with everyone in good causes, we do not diminish our own identity. Instead, we strengthen it. My experience with the Wesley Theological Seminary community in Washington, D.C., has convinced me that this is true. What began as a casual contact led to Wesley's co-sponsoring a preview of the PBS documentary, *The Mormons,* at the American Film Institute, meetings between Wesley theologians and LDS leaders including a meeting between the seminary's president and the LDS First Presidency, and ongoing dialogue at multiple levels. At each step the barriers of distrust are diminishing and are being replaced by a spirit of camaraderie and mutual respect.

These are the reasons why I stay in the Church. On a variety of levels, the Church learns from its mistakes and continues forward while I do the same. It has its share of problems, as do other Churches, and as we work to resolve, rather than ignore, those problems, we and the Church become better. A balance between a science-based approach to some issues and a faith-based approach to others has helped me realize the vision that many people before me have had of harmonizing the two. John Wesley, for one, stated that his goal was to "unite the pair so long disjoined, knowledge and vital piety."

It Takes Many Villages

Mary Lythgoe Bradford

Whenever I'm asked why I'm a Mormon, my first thought is, "Where else would I go?" The Church is my village and my home.

I attended another Church while staying in Eyeries, a village in southwest Ireland, for several months over a three-year period. The Catholic congregation welcomed me, even inviting me to sing in the choir. One of the bachelor farmers complimented me on my no-drinking-or-smoking clean living, adding that he himself had "never touched the drink." He recited the pledge he took as a twelve-year-old. I replied that I, too, had taken a pledge called the Word of Wisdom. I recited a few lines for him. I enjoyed going to Church there, especially since meetings were only about forty-five minutes long.

In my mind the priest was an Irish version of the late Lowell Bennion, whom I so admired all my life. Lowell was the LDS Institute director at the University of Utah and humanitarian whose emphasis was on service to the needy. The Irish priest had trained young men and boys to build homes for the elderly at a previous parish. He gave me a blessing by crossing himself, then laying his hands on my head: "I bless you that you will always have the spirit of Christ in your life."

These experiences did not convert me to Catholicism. Like the historian D. Michael Quinn, I am a DNA Mormon. The Church belongs to me and I to it. I don't intend to leave. Sometimes I feel that the Church is leaving me, but I intend to stick around anyway. I am comforted by the thought that the Church structure we know is a temporal plan. For now, I need some structure in my life. I may not need so many strictures, but I need the association with people in the Church. In the journey that is my life, the most amazing friends and family have been nearby to succor me, accompany me, advise and nourish me. Although I have friends from outside the Church, my really deep bonds have come through Church connections.

Childhood

I was imprinted with LDS convictions as a child when I ran freely over my dad's little acre in East Mill Creek, outside of Salt Lake City. It was our food chain during the Great Depression. We never felt deprived. We ate fresh fruits and vegetables from our garden and meat from the calves or pigs Dad killed once a year. We drank milk from our own cows, Daisy and Buttercup. From my mother, Lavinia Mitchell Lythgoe, I inherited a love for the printed word and the arts. From my father, Leo Lythgoe, I inherited a love for good hard work and the great outdoors. From them both, I came to love the gospel of Jesus Christ. Neither of my parents was educated past the tenth grade, but they supported their children as we chose to pursue higher education.

Through school classes and Church dances, I found I loved books and stories. While others played kickball during grade-school recess, I gathered a little circle of fans and read them my stories. In my early years, I sensed that the parables of Jesus and the stories in the Bible were more convincing than sermons. (The fact that I have not fulfilled my childhood and teenage dream of becoming a fiction writer is partly due to the fact that it was educated out of me and partly because the stories published by writers like Virginia Sorensen were more exciting than anything I could dream up.) The diary I kept from ages thirteen to twenty-two shows that those years were filled with delightful experiences, encouraging teachers, loyal friends, and Church leaders who seemed devoted to my development. In the ward, I learned to give a speech, teach a lesson, write and act in plays and skits, and tend to children. My two younger brothers, Tom and Dennis, and my late-arriving sister, Gaye, were my constant companions.

University

The University of Utah was another kind of village where I signed up for classes at the Institute of Religion under Lowell Bennion, George Boyd, and T. Edgar Lyon. These dovetailed with my classes across the street at the university. I remember thinking, "I am living a charmed life. I want to write about it someday."

As I reflect on those years, I echo Laurel Thatcher Ulrich's words at a commencement speech in which she said her life was anchored by Dr. William Mulder at the university and by Lowell Bennion across the street at the institute. Hats off to them and the other fine professors who helped me earn an M.A. in English and gave me the skills for a lifetime of learning. My great teachers used the Socratic method and asked meaningful questions, which I found more important than memorizing answers. Brother Bennion once wrote on the board: "What is your philosophy of life?" We shallow students had no idea what that might mean. We parroted clichés we had heard in Church while he showed us how superficial our answers were.

Brother Bennion criticized the approach sometimes taken by teachers who seem to ask, "What am I thinking?" instead of "What are YOU thinking?" Life is not a giant *Jeopardy!* game where we are expected to read the minds of our leaders and parrot a response. I believe that the ability to ask questions from deep within the soul leads us to understanding and faith.

Great Adventures

My first full-time job took me to Brigham Young University, where I taught English with another group of creative thinkers—Bruce Clark, Marden Clark, Clinton Larsen, Jeannette Morrell, Leonard Rice, and Orea Tanner, to name a few. I was happy and stimulated in my work but unhappy in Church. In my ward I was a "Special-Interest" or unmarried member with the calling of assistant roll-taker in one of my ward's several Gospel Doctrine classes. I took to traveling to Salt Lake City nearly every Sunday, so friends and family there thought I was attending Church in Provo while the Provoans believed I was in Church in Salt Lake. I was going inactive and nobody realized it—not even I.

Luckily, I began to date someone I had known at the University of Utah who was then teaching economics at BYU while finishing his Ph.D. from Harvard: Charles Henry Bradford, or "Chick," as everyone called him. We had similar backgrounds, the same basic worldview. We held slightly different political views—he a Republican, I a Democrat—but this was before today's polarization into blues and reds. We blended well. We were purple. Power to the Purple!

After our marriage in 1957, I was immediately called as Gospel Doctrine teacher. A few weeks later we accepted with alacrity the opportunity for Chick to work for Senator Wallace Bennett in the U.S. Congress. What a great adventure! Marriage saved me from inactivity and plunged me into the vortex of child-rearing and ward and stake activities. The Arlington, Virginia, ward became my next village. The ward had an impressive history. Its founders built the chapel with their own hands. We thus joined a group of young couples who reared our children together and, because our parents were not nearby, became our own family.

The ward was a healthy mixture of students and government professionals who were readers and thinkers, determined to benefit from the advantages of living near the nation's capital. The Mormons were strong in the Church, and we decided we liked the region despite dire warnings from our Utah family and friends who spoke of the impossibility of rearing Mormon children "in the East." Some expected us to return home to Zion as soon as we could, but we believed we were already in our own Zion.

Dialogue

When Eugene England and friends founded *Dialogue: A Journal of Mormon Thought* in 1966, I volunteered. I saw my support for the journal as part of being "anxiously engaged in a good cause and do[ing] many things of [my] own free will" (D&C 58:27)—a principle I had been taught in my youth. The Church's in-house organs couldn't print all the fine work we young people wanted to write. My involvement put me back in touch with former school friends and colleagues. It was a yeasty time when all kinds of issues were waiting to be questioned.

Gene started me out on my career as a personal essayist when he asked me to write a regular section in the journal. I had no idea that ten years later I would become *Dialogue*'s first female editor at exactly the time when the women's movement was heating up in this country. I have to thank

Bob Rees for "calling" me to be the editor. He remains a friend and brother. I was already in my forties when I became the editor but was still wonderfully naïve. Imagine my surprise upon learning that, speaking from deep within my cozy cocoon, I was now an "alternative voice" in the Church. When I went to Salt Lake City to keep an appointment with the Church Historian, he refused to see me. "I refuse to talk to the editor of *Dialogue*," he said. I was also refused as a speaker at the BYU women's conference by Dallin Oaks, who said: "We can't have just anybody speaking here." I was acquainted with Elder Oaks and knew he had written for *Dialogue,* so his response surprised me. After I had published an article in the *Ensign* on Mormons in Washington, D.C., an editor there said if he had known I was to become *Dialogue*'s editor, he would not have published my article. Whenever I think of this response, I smile, knowing that my article now resides in the cornerstone of the Washington Temple. I am amazed at policies like these. We are all Church members. Why can't leaders sit down and discuss the issues that threaten to divide us?

During my years as editor (1976–1982), I worked with a well-grounded board of editors and a staff for whom no task was too small or too large. While I was still with *Dialogue*, blacks received the priesthood, the Church became more international, women spoke out about their rights and responsibilities, and important parts of Mormon intellectual history came to light. Although the so-called Camelot under Leonard Arrington closed down, professional history writing continued. Lester Bush, associate editor during my tenure, followed his groundbreaking article on blacks in the Church with significant studies of birth control and other subjects. We celebrated the Church's sesquicentennial and published the first papers delivered at conferences of the Mormon History Association and Association for Mormon Letters.

We cooperated with other independent publications such as *Sunstone* and *Exponent II*, exchanging articles and advice.

This was exciting work, which I somehow did while my bishop-husband ran the ward and my children grew up. Professionally, I consulted with government agencies on their writing and led workshops on editing and speaking, a position that came to me through my Mormon network. When it was time to move the journal to Utah under Jack and Linda Newell and Lavina Fielding Anderson, we knew it was strong enough to survive. Its fortieth anniversary was celebrated in 2006.

After my *Dialogue* sojourn, I was entrusted with the life of my mentor and teacher, Lowell Bennion, whose biography I wrote. Thanks to *Dialogue* and the editing advice of wonderful friends such as Gene England, Lavina Anderson, and Emma Lou Thayne, I was able to publish the story of his life just before he died in 1995.

Family and Friends

A reporter once asked Esther Peterson, that great and famous activist from Utah, what advice she would give young women wanting a career in public service. She answered, somewhat surprisingly, "Marry the right man." Chick's unfailing support of everything I tried to do was my strongest pillar of faith. When he passed away in 1991, my ward village, along with my friends in Utah and elsewhere, mourned with me, comforting me during the stages of grief. My three children, Steve, Lorraine, and Scott, along with their twelve children, have among them some of Chick's qualities and when I am with them I don't miss him as much.

My mourning took me to Ireland, that green, grieving land, accompanied by strong women friends. One of these, Sue Booth Paxman, former editor of *Exponent II*, decided to

Not far from the writers' retreat in Eyeries, Ireland, is the Drombeg stone circle, aligned to the winter solstice sunset and once used for funerary purposes. © *Corbis Images*

settle in Ireland. As Sue Booth-Forbes, she opened a writers' and artists' retreat in a little paradise in southwest Cork. She and the people I met there created a village much like my childhood one, which was the perfect spot for me to write and heal. Sue is one of the many friends who have stayed with me through darkness and light. They have given me advice and shelter through long nights of grief and laughed me out of depression. They have helped me rear my children and publish my work. Besides the women I have mentioned, a long line of men, including the mentors and colleagues I have already named, has opened doors for me to both friendship and understanding. It gives lie to the belief that a man and woman cannot be true friends. They can!

Now I am living in my last village. Seven years ago I sold my house in Arlington and moved twenty miles away into a gated retirement community near my daughter. What I thought would be a peaceful old age devoted to writing my memoirs has proved just as challenging as my other sojourns, partly because I am suddenly a widow in a Church of young married people. Shades of Special Interest! If ever I would leave the Church, it would be out of sheer boredom. One source of frustration at Church comes from the deadening influence of assigning subjects to speakers—usually the same subject each week to all the speakers. Though some are experienced enough to turn any topic into a stimulating sermon, most simply resort to a computer index of suitable quotations, thereby losing the personal touch. Lowell Bennion's way of organizing—choosing a topic dear to your heart, then supporting it with scriptures, experience, and prayer—is lost. I used to look forward to the quirky, humorous, personal experiences we heard in people's homilies.

In spite of this, I remain grateful to the structure of the Church, through which I have experienced spiritual blessings, beginning with a healing blessing administered to me at the age of three weeks. Just home from the hospital, I had contracted pneumonia and was turning blue. The doctor had given up on me. My mother recorded in her diary that Bishop Howick stopped in and performed a healing miracle—I was a miracle baby. Since then I have received many priesthood blessings that, if they did not heal me, gave me the courage to carry on. When I was a freshman at the University of Utah, my mother contracted pneumonia. My grandmother ordered me to "take your brothers and pray for your mother." It seemed that my mother's fate depended on it—and she was healed.

Chick suffered from a form of muscular dystrophy. Years into our marriage, he confided that many young women he had dated had expressed fear about bearing children with this hereditary disease. He had taken this to Harold B. Lee, a former school principal and family friend who had become an apostle. Elder Lee gave Chick a blessing and advised him to "be patient" because he would yet meet "a girl with enough faith."

When I became pregnant with our firstborn, Stephen, Chick arranged a meeting with Apostle Lee, who blessed me that my baby would be free of the disease. When sixteen years later Stephen was diagnosed with muscular dystrophy, I had a strange reaction. I recalled that one of Brother Bennion's favorite scriptures was this from Micah: "What does the Lord require of thee, but to do justly, and to love mercy, and to walk humbly with thy God?" (Micah 6:8) From this scripture, I came to understand that justice and mercy were primary qualities and that we should be humble in recognizing that God would walk with us—not ahead or behind us. In meeting the news of Stephen's affliction this way, I became internally satisfied that God would not or could not intervene in the progress of this inherited disease that had already struck generations of worthy Bradfords. That left me with the fact that our child would have to suffer. I took Steve to see a specialist, a doctor who seemed to know of every case in America. She told him: "Look at your father. He is your example of what you can accomplish."

At the time Stephen was meeting with her, I was sitting in the waiting room in deep despair. I thought, "If only I could take this disease on myself." Then Stephen walked smiling into the room. "Mom, there is something I can do," he exclaimed. On our way home, he added, "I believe I chose you and dad in the pre-existence, and I would do it again!" At that moment I knew that even if God had not eradicated the disease, he had given us a great blessing in a son as courageous as his father. Chick was able to turn a disability into an ability—the ability to understand and inspire others.

That the combined prayers of a ward, a stake, and family members could not stop death from taking my husband leaves me in awe at the mysteries of the universe. As I face the end of my life on this earth without my partner, I lean on the gospel of Jesus Christ as I see it joyously lived around me.

Staying in the Community of Christ

William D. Russell

My good friend Scotty Chisholm, the late author of *Following the Wrong God Home*, lived in, of all places, Paradise, Utah. We were students together at Graceland College in Iowa and were proud members of the one true Church of Jesus Christ on the face of the earth. Scotty, who later converted to Catholicism, once visited the Logan Tabernacle with me. He signed the guest register as a Roman Catholic and I signed as an RLDS (now Community of Christ) priest—a member of the Aaronic Priesthood or "lesser priesthood," as it is also called. The senior guide paid the most attention to me, rather than to Scotty. Presumably an RLDS soul would be riper for conversion than someone from the Church our scripture refers to as "the great and abominable church, ... the whore of all the earth." As we were preparing to leave, the guide looked at me, with his back to Scotty, and said, "I hope you will come back to the Church." "I have never been in your Church," I responded. Scotty and I laughed all the way back to Paradise.

Why do I feel an allegiance to my Church, the Community of Christ? To begin with, like Nephi, I was born of goodly parents. My father was a full-time paid minister in the RLDS Church, one of those "hired preachers" the Book of Mormon warns us against. I was raised thinking my Church was the one true Church on the face of the earth, and in my teen years, Church camps and other experiences helped me gain a commitment to take religion and the Church seriously.

I attended our Church college, Graceland, where I graduated with a degree in religion. After graduation, I was offered a job as an editor and writer at Herald House, our Church's publishing house in Independence, Missouri. Soon I began taking courses part-time at Saint Paul (Methodist) Seminary, fifteen minutes from our publishing house. I loved the Bible courses that first year, so the next year I signed up for the History of Christianity sequence. Soon I was into theology, ethics, and Christian social concerns. I eventually earned a Masters of Divinity (M.Div.). I was a part-time student, so it took me six years to complete what takes three years of full-time graduate study.

It was during those years that I began to have serious doubts about the faith claims of my Church. The RLDS Church had published Joseph Smith's "New Translation" of the Bible, which we proudly called the "inspired version." I discovered serious problems with the revisions contained in it. I found that both the New Translation and the King James Version from which it sprang contained inaccuracies that had been illuminated by new discoveries in biblical history and languages and the discovery of ancient manuscripts. I also discovered that Joseph Smith had altered the meaning of some core passages such as Jesus's statement on the cross, "Father, forgive them, for they know not what they do." Joseph added a parenthetical notation "(meaning the Roman soldiers)," limiting Jesus's forgiveness to those who were the instruments but not chief instigators of his crucifixion.

Studying the history of Christianity opened my mind to the great variety of religious meaning and expression in various Christian communities around the world. It also convinced me that the Mormon claim, asserted by both the LDS and Community of Christ Churches, of being a restoration of the original New Testament Church was demonstrably false. At Seminary, the Sociology of Religion was probably the most important single course I took. Reading books like H. Richard Niebuhr's *Social Sources of Denominationalism* and Liston Pope's *Millhands and Preachers* helped me understand that religions arise out of a cultural context and are shaped by that context.

Courses on Christian ethics and Christian social concerns gave me a greater awareness of the religious significance of social and political issues. I became strongly convinced that the gospel is relevant to the big issues of the day, and I wrote editorials in our official publications, as well as letters in the *Kansas City Star* and *Independence Examiner,* on civil rights issues. As a result, I was picketed for three days at our Herald House editorial offices and our 1966 World Conference. The signs read, "The commies just love Wm. D. Russell." My pastor was equally convinced that I was a Communist. That's one reason why I was an adult Aaronic Priesthood holder for so long.

I was disappointed with my Church during this time. The Church didn't appear ready to modify its interpretation of scripture, its understanding of history, or its belief that we were the true Church. Worst of all, our leaders were relatively unconcerned about the Civil Rights Movement and other social and political issues that had clear moral implications. The RLDS Church and the Southern Baptists were the two largest denominations in the Kansas City area without involvement in the Kansas City Council on Religion and Race, a council composed of Protestant, Catholic, and Jewish leaders from the metropolitan area. The LDS Church was not involved either. The executive secretary of the council, George Laurent, asked me to attend the meetings as an

RLDS observer, hoping I could get our Church involved. I was unsuccessful.

In 1966 the council decided to adopt a project in which we would go door-to-door and ask people to sign a Good Neighbor Pledge that when they sold their homes they would not discriminate on the basis of race. I was saddened when only one of the three members of the RLDS First Presidency signed, and it wasn't President W. Wallace Smith. Only one of the three members of the Presiding Bishopric signed, and it wasn't Presiding Bishop G. Leslie DeLapp. Only four of our twelve apostles signed. About that time I learned from a reliable source that President Smith had compared me to the Reverend Martin Luther King, which I thought put me in good company! But he thought we were Communists.

When I was nearly finished with my degree work at Saint Paul, I was offered a position on the faculty in religion at Graceland. I thought Graceland would be my last stop in the Church because I assumed that if I left Graceland I would be in some location where the Church members would be conservative in their interpretation of the Church's history, scripture, theology, and ethical obligations and I would be an outcast. While I was in Independence and Lamoni, I found the Church was dominated by a conservative leadership but that there was a significant core of liberals I could rely on for support. Although I was teaching religion at Graceland, I avoided getting heavily involved in the local congregation. I often attended the worship services on campus because there were more like-minded people there.

When I was invited to speak in rural congregations, I accepted out of a sense of duty. Sometimes I thought, as I took the stand to preach, "What the heck am I doing here?" But gradually the Church changed its position on some issues in a direction I approved of. The Church became more supportive of civil rights for blacks and of nonviolence in the face of the country's involvement in Vietnam. The faculty at Graceland, the staff at the religious education department at Church headquarters, and Church Historian Dick Howard gradually convinced a significant number of the leadership that we should re-think our stands on scripture, history, theology, and social ethics. The Church's reluctance to become involved in the Civil Rights Movement may have been influenced by Joseph Smith III's revelation which became Section 116 of our Doctrine and Covenants. The revelation approved ordination of African Americans but included the language, "Be not hasty in ordaining members of the Negro race to the priesthood."

In 1970 five of us at Graceland began publishing a quarterly journal entitled *Courage: A Journal of History, Thought, and Action* which was consciously modeled after *Dialogue: A Journal of Mormon Thought.* I wrote an editorial in the *Saints' Herald* when the first issue of *Dialogue* came out, praising it and especially applauding an article by Frances Lee Menlove called "The Challenge of Honesty." In *Courage* we took positions which seemed radical at the time but later became the positions of the Church. In 1970 *Courage* endorsed the ordination of women, a position the Church adopted in 1984. In 1971 we endorsed open communion, which the church adopted in 1994. We criticized our method of succession in the presidency, arguing that our lineal succession was as bad as the LDS tradition wherein the senior apostle becomes the prophet. At the 1996 World Conference, Wallace B. Smith called W. Grant McMurray to lead the Church and thus ended our lineal descent in the office of Church president.

In *Courage*, we also contended that issues like peace and human rights should be central gospel concerns. The 1984 revelation that called for the ordination of women added that the soon-to-be-built temple in Independence would be "dedicated to the pursuit of peace, reconciliation, and healing of

The purpose of the Community of Christ temple in Independence, Missouri, was outlined in the same 1984 revelation that gave priesthood to women. Photograph by Joseph Sohm, ca. 1995. © *Corbis Images*

the spirit." These shifts in emphasis in the Church caused me to become more actively involved. It was not just the shift in our approach to scripture, history, and theology that quickened my involvement. Following my divorce in 1986, I found my brothers and sisters in the Church, as well as the leaders, wonderfully supportive, contrary to the experience of many divorcés in the past. Some of my LDS friends were also supportive, especially Lavina Fielding Anderson and Melvin Smith. When asked to preach after the divorce, I discovered that I now felt like I had something to say when I stepped behind the pulpit to proclaim the Word. I had gone through great pain, and now I had gained some new perspectives on life and the nature of the gospel and the call for unconditional love.

One important influence along the way was my involvement in Graceland's annual singles reunion. It was wonderful to find people who loved and accepted everyone whether they were lovable or not. Everyone was divorced, widowed, or had suffered the ostracism that comes from never having married in our couples-oriented society. I discovered that in the RLDS singles community, and especially at our annual six-day reunion, we were truly a community of Christ.

In 1997 I met and married Lois Beach. Not long afterward, we attended a weekend retreat in Chicago of the RLDS-oriented Gay and Lesbian Acceptance group (GALA). When I walked into the room, I found about a half-dozen of the best students I had ever taught, who were also among the nicest, most moral, most Christian human beings I will ever know. I found the GALA community to be a community of Christ where unconditional love prevails. I think its members are more loving and spiritual because of the ostracism they have experienced. Instead of marginalizing such members, we should make them bishops, stake presidents, and apostles.

If the Church had not changed its direction, I would not

be actively involved in it today. I stayed and have become more active today than ever before. I think the key was that the Church I was raised in was too heavily focused on Joseph Smith and not on Jesus Christ. We did so because it served our pride to think we were more blessed than other people in the world. Reinhold Niebuhr called pride the original sin. Now I think the question of whether a Church is "true" is an absurd concept. No institution is fully good. No book is fully true, not even a book alleged to be the most perfect one ever written. No pope, no prophet, no archbishop is perfect. Ambiguity reigns everywhere, in Churches and in society.

It used to be that we saw Jesus through Joseph's eyes and considered the Book of Mormon and revelations of Joseph to have come directly from Jesus. I personally find the revelations to be at variance with the portraits we see of Jesus from first-century sources in the New Testament. Joseph Smith is a secondary, nineteenth-century source, and his understanding of Jesus was filtered to us through his nineteenth-century eyes. Now, in the Community of Christ, we try to see Joseph through Jesus's eyes. In doing so, we have frankly not always liked what we have seen. We have recognized, as President McMurray said in his Mormon History Association lecture in Kirtland in 2003, that Joseph Smith was a flawed human being like the rest of us. Our Church Historian, Mark Scherer, told *Newsweek* that in polygamy Joseph Smith found a theological rationale for adultery. Other Church leaders have said similar things.

After forty-one years of being what Latter-day Saints call an Adult Aaronic, at the age of sixty-one I received a promotion to the greater priesthood, named after some little-heard-of guy who was called Melchizedek. In recent years I have served on World Church committees on racism, human rights, and peace and justice. I am the Peace and Justice Coordinator for our mission center in Iowa.

I also preach regularly. This Sunday I will speak at our Salt Lake City congregation and next Sunday I will speak at my former congregation in Independence, Missouri, where I was once discriminated against because my pastor thought I was a Communist. My first wife disliked the Church intensely. Lois, my current wife, holds the priesthood and is the worship chair for our church in Lamoni, which is the largest congregation in Iowa.

Therefore, I suspect I will remain in the Community of Christ until the undertaker arrives. At my funeral, please don't assign me to heaven. I have no idea whether such a nice fuzzy place exists. I just hope I can muddle through the rest of this life without screwing up too much. I leave the rest in God's hands.

A Surgeon's Overwhelming Gratitude

Fred Christensen

A fourth-generation Latter-day Saint, I am a great-grandson of John Pack, whose likeness is on the *This Is the Place* monument at the mouth of Emigration Canyon. Pack was in the advance party that entered the Salt Lake Valley in 1847 a few days before Brigham Young arrived. When he was an old man, the last of Pack's eight wives bore him a daughter, Flora, who was my grandmother. Those of us with such heritages are sometimes called genetic Mormons, but that alone would not be reason enough to remain in the Church. Sustained commitment, rather than passive acceptance, is required.

When I finished my mission, my mission president, Henry D. Taylor, knowing I was planning to enter medical school, said, "There is a good chance we will lose you if you go into medicine. We lose most of you scientists." That was generally true at the time, but I couldn't fathom that possibility. I had just completed two years of the most intense indoctrination one could imagine, and I took his caution as a passing comment rather than a serious observation. Although remaining in the Church has been a struggle at times, having passed my seventh decade as an active, committed member and feeling as I do now, I would be able to say to President Taylor, "I think that is highly unlikely."

The subject of religion never came up in medical school because it was more or less irrelevant. However, the thought processes, the avenues to understanding, are in opposition to those of religious discourse. In religion, understanding is hierarchical. In the Latter-day Saint Church, the thinking derives from agreed-upon conclusions. In medical school the thinking is deductive. One day Dr. Hillman Castle presented a patient with edematous (swollen) ankles, rales (rattling sound) in his lungs, and difficulty breathing. He looked down the roster of students and, stopping at my name, said, "Christensen, what's wrong with him?" "He is in congestive heart failure," I said and waited for the expected approval of my acumen. Dr. Castle was a former World War II fighter pilot. "That response is like dropping bombs from twenty thousand feet. Everything looks like the enemy from that altitude. If you came down a little closer, you would find you're bombing children on a field trip." He was looking for a differential diagnosis, the different possibilities and order of likelihood. I have tried to adopt that same reasoning process with issues in the Church, an approach that may smack of unorthodoxy to some other Church members. In the conflict between honesty and loyalty, I am increasingly more comfortable with honesty.

Settling in Arizona after I completed my neurosurgical residency, I was asked to teach the Gospel Doctrine class and my deductive teaching style stimulated interesting class participation. However, I was advised to stick closer to the lesson manual. I didn't do so and was eventually replaced by a new teacher. After a short hiatus, I taught the young adult class and tried to be less controversial. My next assignment was teaching the seasoned older men of the high priests quorum. I resumed giving lessons that looked for alternative explanations. After several years I was asked to become the high priests group leader with the provision that I not teach the class. My questioning approach, ideal in medicine, left unresolved issues in religion that unsettled the class. More than that, it challenged some fundamental propositions taught in the Church. In the following paragraphs I would like to explore some of those issues and explain how I resolved them.

In the Bible, disease is seen as the effect of supernatural power. Seizures and schizophrenia were thought to result from being possessed by evil spirits. Plagues were God's vengeance. We see how so often we use God to fill in the gaps in our understanding. As science increases our understanding, the role of God tends to diminish. In any case, one day while in medical school, I was asked as part of a Church assignment to go to a hospital with another brother and administer to some members who were sick. In the first room we visited, we met a young quadriplegic on a Stryker frame who had minimal use of his arms and no use of his legs. He had been that way for the past year. Even though the priesthood has the power to move mountains and heal the sick, I was quite sure this young man's paralysis could not be reversed. It was science in conflict with religion. I asked my companion if he would give the blessing, relieving me of the conflict I felt. In my thirty years as a neurosurgeon and priesthood holder, I have never seen a hopeless medical problem reversed by a priesthood administration. Medical conditions with predictably favorable outcomes seem to do the best.

I don't believe that disease can be simply exorcized by the power of the priesthood. This does not mean I consider administering to the sick to be a useless exercise. There is more to healing sick people than excising tumors, vaccinating against contagious diseases, and prescribing the right antibiotic. One's mental attitude can have a measurable physical and psychological effect. More than a simple placebo, blessings can produce measurable physical changes. No one questions whether hypnotism can temporarily eliminate pain. I have likewise seen patients become completely pain-free after a priesthood blessing. Patients with positive attitudes tend to get well faster after major surgery, and a priesthood administration often gives patients that positive outlook, the feeling of divine assistance. Thus, I still believe in the power of the priesthood to heal the sick, but I no longer believe that it can reverse hopeless situations.

It has been twenty years since I believed the Book of Mormon was a historical record of people who once lived in the Americas. The strange description of Jaredite boats, the many anachronisms, the inconsistency of correlating known population expansion rates with the book's census numbers, passages from the King James Bible that are presented out of their historical context, and the lack of supporting archeological evidence (even though we were once assured that Mayan ruins were evidence of Book of Mormon peoples) raise too many doubts. Based on the folklore of the early nineteenth century, it was a plausible story; but as our understanding of archeology has unfolded, I have come to see the book as myth. The recent DNA evidence is simply one more piece of evidence discounting the book as a historical record. The revisionist historian's limited geography sounds like the story of Cinderella's slipper in that if you cut off a big toe here and a heel there, it fits just fine. That the entire Amerind population was Israelite was once universally taught in the Church and believed by my generation. To many this would seem an insurmountable hurdle to continuing belief in the Church. Initially I suppose I felt betrayed and wanted to share my anger with others. With time I have come to have a more mature understanding of the Church. Were the leadership to declare the Book of Mormon metaphorical, I feel confident the Saints would not suddenly renounce their membership. The history of the American Indian was only peripheral to the main reason my ancestors were baptized. They joined in order to belong to a community of people who relied on God's assistance.

The Book of Mormon is not the only thing we hold sacred that I consider myth. In the secular world, our judicial system favors the wealthy, while the confidence Mormons place in our democratic government seems most firm among those who have had the least exposure to governments. Likewise, the Bible is less than accurate history, with a mythical creation and a world-encompassing flood. All of this has led me to conclude that we are judged better by the myths we believe in than by the realities we live. We fall short of the ideal, but we maintain our illusions because they express what we hope to become, what we hope would be true. The Book of Mormon has wonderfully inspiring stories that reflect the kind of God I believe in. It includes the messages of Christ, and they are the core of my religious guidance. Whatever its non-historical origin, its ethical guidelines are, for the main, a valuable anchor.

Several years ago, on a trip to Salt Lake City for the first time in forty years, I visited the neighborhood where I was raised. Mr. Kissel's barbershop was gone, as was the Fix-It-Shop which had become an emission testing station. Our house on Millbrook Road had been torn down, replaced by a newer residence I could only see as ugly. Change is the only thing that is certain. We are short-term custodians, even of ideas, in this life. Is it any surprise that some defining doctrines of the Church have changed? Is that a threat to my membership? Polygamy, the bedrock doctrine of early Mormonism, the practice for which my ancestors sacrificed everything, is now considered a sin. My grandmother Christensen, daughter of a polygamous marriage, was put out to hire as a house servant when her father died because this failed social experiment had produced an inadequate economic base for the extended family. Were the government to reverse the laws against polygamy tomorrow as unfair restrictions on personal freedom, it is unlikely the Church would sanction the practice. We have renounced the highest form of celestial marriage. We have renounced the communal economics we called the United Order. We have reversed ourselves on the gathering of the ten tribes, the stain of a dark skin, and advice against birth control. We have softened the temple ceremony and accommodated the temple garment to more modern styles. We seldom mention such spiritual gifts as speaking in tongues or casting out devils that once were prominent practices in the Church. Somehow we have managed to adjust to the changes in seemingly eternal principles, revelations, and practices as required by changing conditions. Without such social and doctrinal changes, we would be condemned to Darwinian extinction. I am not threatened by doctrinal change; I am only disappointed that it often takes place so slowly, especially when change seems obvious and inevitable.

Not long ago I sat in Church contemplating the congregation. The missionaries were speaking with tunnel-vision platitudes and naïve sincerity, and I thought, "How fortunate we and they are." There will be plenty of time in the future for them to rebel, if we can only get them through the next ten years maintaining this sweet optimism. I thought of the misdirected religious zeal of the al-Qaeda suicide bombers. Some in the congregation had serious financial problems and others serious health problems. I could find troubled issues in each person's life if I probed deeply enough. What they had in common, however, the one reason they had congregated, was that they wanted to be better people. What a wonderful mission statement! I thought, "I love these people. I want to be with them." This is the reason people join the Church. It is the desire to be part of a community they look up to, to associate with high ideals. It has little to do with doctrinal issues that in reality most understand poorly. The strength of the Church is its social organization, not its doctrinal philosophy that is forever changing. We are fundamentally a social organization with doctrinal issues giving us something to talk about. Mine was a slow climb over the hurdle of coming to understand this, and having passed over it, it has relieved much of the tension I felt about messages from the pulpit I disagreed with.

There is another reason I remain in the Church. This may be the most important of all. As a neurosurgeon, my relationship with patients has been based on trust. Many times when I took patients to surgery, they trusted me with their lives. It would have been easy and financially rewarding to liberalize my assessment of a patient's needs and operate when time alone might produce a similar outcome. Since it is simple to up-code procedures and multiply insurance payments, no one would have found this out, but there was always a voice that said, "I am watching you." There were female patients and lonely nurses who tried to tempt me to compromise my standards, but the same voice said, "Don't go there." How different my life might have been had I not had the refining influence of the gospel and my allegiance to a Church community. Corporate America has seen what happens when there is no moral compass. I want my children, my grandchildren, and many others to hear the same voice I heard.

I am filled with overwhelming gratitude for having survived seventy years without a major health problem. I am grateful that I was not born into poverty, that I found a mate I adore more every day. I can only ask, "Why me?" Maybe I could have done all this without the Church, I don't know. But I believe the Church has been a contributing factor to my good life. I am disturbed by much of the Church's orthodoxy, but I have managed to discount it in the balance. I think there is room in the Church for differing views. At least, I hope others who have views like mine are consoled that I remain, while those whose views are different continue to tolerate me.

I Always Intended to Leave

Lael Littke

Someone sent me an e-mail once in a mass mailing, but it seemed to have been written for me. It said, "Don't criticize the Church. If it were perfect, you couldn't belong to it." How true that is! The knowledge that neither I nor the Church is perfect is one of the things that allows me to stay. Ironically, since the age of thirteen, I've thought I might leave someday. I know where the idea began. When I was a Beehive Girl back in Mink Creek, Idaho, our Beekeeper conducted a survey one evening by asking each of the six girls in my class what we wanted to be when we grew up. I was, I think, the fifth to answer. The first four said a wife and mother. When it came my turn, I said, "I want to be a writer."

I don't know if Sister Anderson gasped or if I just felt that she did, but everyone looked at me as she said, "Well, don't you want to be a wife and mother?" I was obviously not bright enough to have caught on that this was not a multiple choice survey. "Of course I do," I said. "Can't I be a wife and mother *and* a writer?"

I don't remember what Sister Anderson said then, but I got the impression that there was no way I could do both and still be a good Mormon. So I decided that if the Church was

The world moves slowly in Mink Creek, Idaho. This photograph of a typical landscape in the nearby Preston area was taken by Scott T. Smith in the 1980s.

© Corbis Images

going to make me choose between the two, it would be no contest. I would leave the Church.

In the meantime, we were learning to dance in *Mewchull,* as we called the Mutual Improvement Association, and there were a number of cute boys in my ward. Since this was a tiny farming community and not a lot going on, and since the Church held at least one dance a month—sometimes more if a special occasion came along (and even a square dance now and then)—I decided I'd stay. The boys got cuter as time went on. I was a nerd and misfit—shallow, frivolous, flaky— but I was a good dancer and the cute boys liked to dance with me. So I decided to stay until I got to college. There would be a lot of people there I could hang out with when I no longer needed the Church.

However, when I got to Utah State University, it was over-whelming to be fresh off the farm among so many people. I went over to the Institute of Religion where I felt more famil-iar and began attending classes and activities. There were so many cute boys at the Institute. Some of them liked to dance with me and took me to the Institute and college dances. I had some dates with non-LDS guys, but I didn't know what to talk to them about if we didn't discuss our Book of Mormon classes or whether or not we were going to go on missions. So I stuck around a little longer.

I graduated in education and English. Teaching in a small Utah town wasn't my aspiration, and since I was going to leave the Church after all, I went to Denver where one of my best girlfriends was already established. I wanted to be a career girl. In a city like that, I wouldn't need my old social crutches. Little did I know that Denver would be even more overwhelming than college. While I got acquainted with peo-ple at work, they were mostly married. I ended up going with my girlfriend to the Denver First Ward, which was jam-packed with cute airmen from Lowry Air Force Base and college students. They liked to dance with me. "Oh well," I thought. "There'll be time to leave later."

While there, I met George Littke—a handsome returned missionary who wanted to be a college professor. I liked him and he liked me. I was torn when it came to the idea of marriage. I still had a fierce ambition to be a writer. I had been taking extension classes sponsored by Denver University and was making progress there. I didn't know whether I could pursue a career if I were a good Mormon wife and mother. I remembered my Beehive leader's reaction all too well.

George said he wanted a wife who had her own interests. That was reassuring, but I was still troubled. One time when we drove home to Idaho and Utah to meet each other's folks, I made an appointment at USU with an Institute teacher I had liked a lot. I told him my dilemma. Could I be both a writer and a good Mormon wife and mother? He leaned back in his chair. He steepled his fingers. He smiled beatifically. He said, "Oh Lael, once you hold your first baby in your arms, you'll forget all about that stuff." That *stuff*? I stomped out of that interview and told George I was leaving the Church. He said okay, then asked if I would wait until after we get married so that I wouldn't complicate things with our parents. I said I guessed I could. "I mean married in the temple," he said. Well, I was still a member in good standing. I attended meetings faithfully. I paid my tithing. It seemed to mean a lot to him, so we got married in the Logan temple.

We were happy living in Denver, but five months after our wedding, George accepted a fellowship to finish his doctorate at New York University in New York City! Back on the farm, I'd dreamed of living in New York and being a writer. There is a song I like that says, "New York, New York, a helluva town. The Bronx is up, but the Battery's down. The people ride in a hole in the groun'. New York, New York, it's a helluva town!"

I loved it. I was hired as a secretary at an insurance lobbying group on Madison Avenue. The work was interesting. I thought that surely now I could leave the Church. However, the people from my office were spread out from Long Island to New Jersey and there wasn't much chance to make real friends. I went with George to the Manhattan Ward, housed in the shabby but beloved old building on West 81st Street. What exciting people we met there! I didn't want to leave the church just yet. It was too much fun. I got involved in shows that Thor Nielsen was putting on and in full-scale productions of *The Messiah* at Christmas. I was asked to teach the literature lessons in Relief Society. I began writing my own shows for the ward using the fantastic talents of the ward members. No, this wasn't the time to leave just yet.

Nine years passed. We had a daughter, Lori. Then finally George finished his Ph.D. except for writing his dissertation and he accepted a position teaching political science at California State University Los Angeles. We moved to southern California amid dark hintings from our New York friends that we would hate it. Within days we knew we had come to the right place and that I could now leave the Church. There was so much to do in California, from the mountains to the desert to the sea. The Monterey Park ward building was just a few blocks away. Our next-door neighbor was an elderly LDS widow who needed a ride to Church. We had a little daughter who loved Primary. One thing led to another, and there I was, still in the pews.

That's how it's gone all my life, even during my strongly feminist years in the seventies and early eighties. There was always another roadshow to write or fun lesson to teach or party to go to with the delightful friends we met in our various wards. I have close friends outside the Church, but the ones who understand me best are within it. I've had in mind since age thirteen to find a new lifestyle, but I never will. What would be left of me if I cast aside the Church and all it has been to me for these many decades? I'd be a pale shadow of myself. My whole foundation is built on it. All my supporting pillars are derived from what it taught me. I find that what I have become has been because of the Church and the associations I've had through it. The Church is my culture, the tribe I belong to.

The Church helped me develop my writing talents, too. The first story I sold back in the sixties was published in the old *Relief Society Magazine*. I progressed to writing novels published by both national and LDS publishers. My inclination for writing musical shows, which is what my college aptitude tests said I should do, was indulged back in 1968 when I wrote a full-length musical for the East Los Angeles Stake Relief Society. Then we moved to the East Pasadena ward where there were restless people like myself—grasshoppers who wanted to sing and dance their way through life. Our ward encouraged us, cherished us, in fact. We formed an unbeatable team in our stake roadshow competition, and I got to influence teenagers through that activity. Dale White, the director of our shows, always sat the kids down on opening night, after they were all dressed up in their costumes with their make-up on and knew their parts and the production numbers perfectly since we'd worked so hard for six weeks. He would say, "Remember how we were at our first rehearsal? Everyone had two left feet. We were awkward and insecure. Compare that with what we feel about ourselves now. We're confident and graceful. We know where to put our feet. What has made the difference?" They'd all yell back, "Hard work!" Then they'd giggle because they'd complained every step of the way and knew what it had taken to stay on.

I had stayed, too. I look back now at that wildly ambitious thirteen-year-old kid I once was and compare her to myself today. Confident some of the time, occasionally knowing where to put my feet, I'm a person who has realized her dream to become a writer, as well as a wife and mother. If I ask what has made the difference, I'd have to say it was the Church. I learned how to work hard on the farm, but I learned how to apply hard work to life through activities and teachings I encountered in the Church.

I haven't mentioned the doctrines, but over the years I've realized that the real reason I stay is because of a belief system I am converted to. I love the gospel of Jesus Christ. From my own experiences with other churches and cultures, I have come to understand that for me, the New Testament gospel is implemented beautifully through the structure of the LDS Church. It's not perfect, but neither am I. That reminds me of a quote from President Hinckley: "Anyone who imagines that bliss is normal is going to waste a lot of time running around shouting that he's been robbed. The fact is that most putts don't drop, most beef is tough, most children grow up to be just people, most successful marriages require a high degree of mutual toleration, and most jobs are more often dull than otherwise. Life is like an old time journey [with] … delays, sidetracks, smoke, dust, cinders, and jolts, interspersed only occasionally by beautiful vistas and thrilling bursts of speed. The trick is to thank the Lord for letting you have the ride." I have loved my ride on the vehicle that is the Church. That's why I stay.

With Neither Blind Faith nor Blind Rejection

Chase Peterson

I believe very much in God and his son Jesus Christ, and I have a relationship with Divinity that works for me, inspires me, guides me, comforts me. That relationship is facilitated by organized religion. If I were asked to draw up an equation balancing the benefits and occasional concerns an individual faces within a group, I would have to say that it is not reducible to merely rational factors. Even so, here is a quick listing of the plusses of my faith.

The gospel of Christ is breathtaking. However, it must be exercised in a real world of real people. Monasteries have their value, I suppose. Even through Christ was an ascetic, he was not cloistered, nor are we. We have a community of human concerns and exercise a personal and communal spirituality. My ward fasted for our grandson, Charlie, who had a progressive, genetic-based muscular paralysis. Perhaps the effort could be said to have failed because Charlie died. Still, he died in the virtual arms of hundreds of Saints who cared for him, and his parents and his grandparents experienced a oneness of life and mortal death and a oneness of caring spirits that is hard to even put into words.

I believe that eternal progression applies to the Church collectively as much as it does to individuals. In my case, do I always progress quickly enough? No, I can be stubborn–deaf and blind–to new truths. Goodness tends to take more time to develop than we might expect. Does the Church always progress quickly enough for some of us? Could the Church have acted sooner in extending the priesthood to blacks? The Church requires the same learning arc, dictated by revelation, and as much reconditioning as the rest of us require individually. I could be wrong, but I suspect that in a similar way we are now painfully working through some issues relating to same-sex relationships. Change is powerful when it is optimistic and full of Christ's love. The Church is seen as both cautious and radical by critics and supporters. I value its capacity to grow with inspiration and revelation, and in such matters, for instance, as birth control; abortion for rape, incest, and the mother's health; and zero tolerance for child abuse, our Church has been much more timely in moving to new attitudes than most other religions. The revelations to Joseph Smith are perhaps the most *radical* religious events of the last two thousand years.

Free agency is a reality that is recognized and respected by the Church. It is a sometimes cumbersome, eruptive, but essential human capacity that frees me to test my faith and enjoy individual spiritual adventures.

Local lay participation helps bring everyone a sense of ownership as they participate in their individual callings. It is a brilliant nineteenth-century application of what we now consider to be a good management philosophy. I am sure participation in Church duties has invariably helped me to grow as much or more than I could ever just *receive*.

The Church advises us to exercise direct access to God and spirituality through prayer, the Holy Ghost, and personal interpretations of scripture in concert with priesthood intercession, all of which I applaud, as Elder Dallin H. Oaks has said in general conference.

My heritage in the Church is strong. I grew up a "Mormon boy," raised in the tenants of the faith. No doubt this helped me as I grew to be an independent adult who came to be simultaneously grateful and challenged by my community of fellow Saints. Even though the other congregants support me, as I do them, we also challenge each other. Through all of this, I remain loyal to the organization of the Church. There is a perpetual balancing of duty to society's will on the one hand and individual conscience on the other, of consensus and independence. This will never be resolved or softened, but I have been helped by people, ideas, and situations as I have also hoped to help.

My parents never smothered me religiously. As I've thought about it, there were some telling experiences in my early life that probably shaped my later direction. For instance, at age ten or twelve, I remember my older sister bristling at a sermon delivered at a stake conference. The speaker seemed quite rigid and unloving in his remarks. My mother smiled and said, "Well, I don't think I needed that but likely someone did." That has always stuck with me as the proper way to view the multiple messages the priesthood is bound to deliver to different members at different times—including when I needed to hear something I might not have asked for.

Another experience that comes to mind is when my father once came home from the Sunday School class he regularly taught in Logan, saying: "Chase, never discount the personal responsibility this Church gives its members to come to their own conclusions. Before I could start today's lesson, Brother Jones stood up and said, Brother Peterson, I have thought and prayed about our discussion last week on the topic of such and such and I have decided that the Lord was right." My father could have censored this man for arrogance in presuming to judge God. But instead, he let the man, who was a janitor of a local bank, come to the point to where he could claim the doctrines of the eternities as his own.

At age fifteen I went away to a private school in New England on a scholarship that somehow came my way. Leaving home prompted me to correspond with my family. My mother told me she would share bits of wisdom she came across as long as I felt free to reject what I wanted and not hold her responsible for them. One such quote was from Albert Schweitzer, the theologian, physician, and organist. Speaking of the interplay of faith and reason, he said that when faced with a difficult problem, one should study it from every side and by every means available, after which one should quiet the mind, pray, and wait for the insight that thought and prayer brought. I have never forgotten that advice or the gentle way in which it was presented to me. I was to come to understand that Schweitzer was describing the Holy Ghost.

Leaving home so young and remaining in New England for fifteen years, I was often the only Mormon my friends knew. I almost felt like I was a "Brigham Young" going east for the weight I felt in carrying the mantle of my religion and Utah's culture on my shoulders. Under those circumstances, if I indulged in any form of teenage rebellion, it was probably to "rebel into," rather than against, Church orthodoxy.

In college I grew to rely more and more on the comfort that can come through personal prayer. In recent years science has found that we grow and remold our brains constantly until the day we die. What could possibly remold our brains in a more constructive way, as preparation for imminent encounters with the world, than prayer in the morning and evening and in-between—perhaps as a regular *conversation* with God. The focused thought on topics of importance and inspiration from Christ when we ask for it—this recurring conversation and meditation—must shape the architecture of the brain and the products of our thinking as our brains listen and learn and heal and develop.

My journey has taken me from a lad in Logan to a grateful husband to Grethe and the father of wonderful children and grandchildren, as well as to semi-retirement as a medical school teacher. The students seem to understand me, and I understand them. It is, for me, a spiritual as well as a temporal exercise to teach medicine. You can call it neuroanatomy, perhaps, but our receptivity and habits have an influence on the outcome of our daily thoughts and acts.

In conclusion, my odyssey was aided and secured by my Church and by my growing in an ever-changing faith. I am grateful for that process and can recommend it to my children and grandchildren with neither smothering insistence nor smug aloofness, with neither blind faith nor blind rejection, but with intense individuality, anchored in free agency and a growing appreciation for my historic and current debt to many good Church leaders and my fellow Saints. These are the reasons why I have chosen to stay—and could not imagine otherwise.

I Stay to Serve and Be Served

Molly Bennion

I was born into a Protestant family and raised Lutheran. Had I been born in the Church, I might have been more disturbed by historical and doctrinal inconsistencies and left. A friend asked me if I would join the Church today if I were learning about it for the first time. My answer was possibly not. It would depend as much on what I learned outside of Mormonism as what I know now, looking at it from the inside.

My parents were Scotch Presbyterian and Lutheran, with a Greek and Emersonian-transcendentalist overlay. My father did not attend Church throughout my youth. He read philosophy and poetry to me to balance what we learned in our Lutheran catechism classes. "To thine own self be true" was his mantra. My grandfather Alexander McLellan emigrated from Scotland. As a child I wore a pin, a crest with the McLellan motto, "Think On." To my father, few sins were greater than letting someone else do your thinking for you. He taught me to study hard and to humbly recognize my dependence on other people's research and thought but never to abdicate the responsibility I had to weigh out the evidence for myself on each question of importance.

I have stayed in the Church as I have watched too many

friends leave. They have left over complaints that I share. Some have disliked such policies and practices as the deceitful campaign to defeat the ERA, attempts to prohibit real scholarship on Church history, surreptitious forays into gay-marriage politics, sour bishops and excommunication of members widely believed to be faithful. These things have been disappointments to me as well. Some people have left because of the absence of female role models or of women's input in major decision making. Some have left out of shear boredom. Some need their spiritual community to be more engaged in seeking answers to troubling questions. Those who feel the need for a vibrant religious community sense a spiritual malaise in our ranks. Some have left because they were offended.

As they have left, I have felt lonely. I dearly miss them. In *Dialogue* in 2006, I wrote that the Church has become the loneliest place I regularly go.[1] A number of people wrote offering friendship and expressing concern for me. I was really touched, but my loneliness is confined to Church and mostly to Church meetings. Most of my close Mormon friends are not in my ward or stake. They never have been. Many friends are not LDS. I am always looking for good friends at Church and this year I have found one, but that is rare.

Frankly, most of the social activities at church bore me or conflict with activities I would rather do. Church classes usually bore me even more. As I said in my *Dialogue* lament, the boredom is more than mind-numbing and exhausting. I come to Church hoping to be refreshed and invigorated, healed from the wounds of a week's work and energized to face the challenges of the next week. Instead I can leave weary, frustrated, demoralized, and hungry, both spiritually and intellectually. Few members show any interest in the intellectual and spiritual questions with which I regularly wrestle. Reading an inspiring book on a quiet Sunday evening at the end of my dock, enveloped by a glorious sky that pulls my spirit upward, is usually far more nourishing than a Church meeting. I have become rather picky in what I will and will not do to help at Church. I will do anything meaningful, but I will not attend useless make-work meetings. I reached sixty this year and feel impatient to learn and serve while I still can. My father once had a photographic memory, and he is now crippled with dementia. Will I be next? I've wasted enough time already. There is simply no time left to waste.

If it is all that bad, why do I stay? I do so because of what I believe and what I do not believe. I stay because gospel principles, which seemed oddly familiar to me from my first exposure but which I took years to consider as I wrestled with the Church's history, still seem true to me. I stay because I have had a few confirming spiritual experiences. I stay because I am also committed to the Church's volunteer structure that provides practical and promising ways for me to become more loving by serving other people. What others believe and do around me is almost irrelevant. To explain, I will return briefly to my upbringing.

In my parents' view of life, the Greek humanist element had the effect of softening the hard-edged Calvinist and Lutheran beliefs about humankind being "a mess" so that they saw human beings as "a work in progress." I have never expected religious leaders to be more than men who are often inspired to do fine deeds but who sometimes do not-so-fine deeds. Sometimes they are noble and sometimes not, but always, like us, each is a work in progress. Even the scriptures are influenced by flawed human hands and are logically imperfect. Sometimes I am disappointed by leaders, but never disillusioned. I have not been forced to lower my expectations because they were always mercifully low! I ever hope for the finest examples of goodness in people. However, I am not derailed when people fall short of the ideal. Sexism, rac-

For inspiration, there is nothing like a good book on a Sunday afternoon, but for Christian service, one has to be among people. Photograph by Monalyn Gracia. © Corbis Images

ism, greed, pettiness, and power-grabbing politics infect all organizations, religious and otherwise.

The God in whom I believe is much less involved in every word and deed of our Church hierarchy than some would assume. Unfortunately, God is also much less involved in my own life than I would like. He could save me from many an error, but he doesn't. He seems rather uninvolved in human life in general. I often feel, as did the author of Lamentations, "You [God] have covered yourself with a cloud so that prayer should not pass through" (3:44). But I don't see another belief system in which God is more involved either. Like the psalmist, I say to God, "Rouse yourself," and I wonder, "Why do you sleep, O Lord?" (44:24-27) Perhaps God is busy with other, more important concerns or perhaps he wants to see how we'll ride without training wheels, but whatever the reasons, I think he inspires on occasion but doesn't control.

I believe in the basic tenets of the LDS Church. I believe in God. I've read the agnostic and atheistic theories that claim we have a psychological need to believe and can't face life without giving it eternal meaning, that spiritual experiences are due to neurological phenomena, and so on. Perhaps the scientists are right. It is true that I cannot even prove the existence of God to one of my sons, let alone to a skeptic. Neither can an unbeliever disprove the existence of God for lack of evidence. To say that all reality is understandable and explicable seems to me narrow and arrogant. We know so little of the workings of the brain and of the metaphysical that I cannot conclude that our current understanding defines the sum total of truth or that we even have the means to acquire all truth. Rather, rational being that I think I am, I believe the Church teaches a reasonable and defensible doctrine conducive to good living both here and in the hereafter. Because I do not expect spiritual experiences, I am probably more profoundly moved when they do happen. I have had several experiences that are difficult to explain but too real to deny. Nor can I deny the spiritual experiences of other people I trust even though I can't prove that their experiences have been authentic, externally stimulated phenomena either.

Inexplicable spiritual truth is real. We simply have to examine it using different tools than we use to look at the physical world. We have to examine spiritual assumptions because we cannot let them become an excuse for superstition or a defense of the ridiculous. In the same vein, faith has to be limited to what seems likely but cannot be tested to our complete satisfaction. The personal nature of spiritual discovery, coupled with the unique set of information and analyses which inform faith, lead me to conclude that I cannot relegate my religious convictions to the dustbin of simple need or neurological responses. I find rationality, order, and goodness in the LDS gospel message. At the risk of further personalizing an already anthropomorphic Mormon God, if I were to design a gospel, it would closely resemble ours. I believe in personal progression. I believe in individual responsibility, in a life that serves as a test and does not require constant divine intervention. I believe in a God confined by principles and conditions which preceded him, notably the existence of evil. I could not believe in a God who created evil. I do not believe in original sin. I do not understand the Atonement, though I have accepted tentative theories which satisfy me for the time.

I believe in the equality of humankind in the eyes of God. The theory of a literal brotherhood and sisterhood is immensely satisfying. It makes sense even if the logistics don't. Universal acceptance of this idea would revolutionize world history. Perhaps I just want to believe we are family, but here again we have a theory consistent with the gospel message of love, hope, and charity that renders life productive and joyful and is compatible with our own experiences.

I believe that ordinances that have eternal meaning have to be made available to everyone who has ever lived. Anything less would strike me as being unjust or unmerciful. Either the Mormon approach is right or ordinances serve only earthly purposes.

It has been suggested that Mormonism requires the trammeling of the mind, the narrowing of inquiries, and the blind acceptance of doctrines and rules. That view is inconsistent with the whole of gospel teaching, particularly with the belief that God has yet to reveal additional truths and that we must seek out all that is virtuous, lovely, and praiseworthy. Neither is it consistent with the Mormon emphasis on individual accountability. It is a convenient position for bureaucratic functionaries who have a controlling bent, but I do not fear bureaucracy any more than I fear my fellow beings. I fear God. We humans drink milk before meat, but we cannot sustain health on a lifetime diet of milk. The hunt for meat takes us into the wilds. I will confidently go on reading what I wish and contributing to forums and journals which herald the value of an honest and vigorous search for truth. I do not care how it appears to others because God knows, and I think blesses, my motives.

I also stay because I believe Joseph Smith was a prophet. I do not believe he had the skill, the materials, or the time to produce his body of work without divine influence. No amount of genius or psychological deviance or alleged plagiarism explains the Book of Mormon for me. I confess I don't even enjoy most of the book. It is militaristic and almost void of the female. I find it less than satisfying in many ways, just as I find the Bible flawed in many ways. I certainly see the hand of man in both. Both compilations are quite confusing, yet both set forth a complex, inspiring, and largely consistent religion.

What about Joseph himself? He was flawed too and some

of his flaws were major. They fit nicely into my belief that even prophets have the capacity for serious error and that God gives us a long rope to hang or save ourselves. Free agency is both the most terrifying and the most reassuring of principles. It is terrifying for the loneliness and responsibility it offers, yet reassuring to know that we matter, that life matters.

I am not just a believer. I am an active member of the Church. I once asked Lowell Bennion why we should attend worship services when the experience is too often unsatisfying. He said, "To serve and to bless, to be served and blessed." That advice has helped me. Long ago I stopped expecting Church to be a place to learn history or theology, a place for an encompassing social life, a place to find social justice, or a place to shortcut the hard work of developing the knowledge and spiritual depth necessary to develop and sustain a testimony of gospel truths. I must find those on my own. Yes, Church is a place to serve and be served, along with the concomitant blessings. There is not much more available at Church, but that's okay. I have regrets because I wish it were otherwise. I am sometimes thrilled to find it is otherwise. But letting go of the expectation has allowed me to participate.

For me, participating is the shortest path to understanding how to internalize Christ-like love. I learn to serve, not because the recipients of my assistance are necessarily worthy or even appreciative—and certainly not because the timing is convenient—but simply because someone is in need. I have learned that classes which are boring to me meet the needs of others. I appreciate the efforts of the struggling teachers who are also learning by doing, just as I am. The Church offers me an opportunity to take advantage of a taxing, imperfect, but brilliant system for meeting human needs and improving human souls.

So I remain doctrinally and spiritually Mormon even

though culturally the Church is not always a comfortable fit. I welcome opportunities to exercise faith and serve others. I continue my search for truth by acting on beliefs rather than simply reading and thinking about them. I try to find strength to live in accordance with faith, and that includes attending worship services and being involved in the LDS community. I think I am a better person for doing so.

Note

1. Molly McLellan Bennion, "A Lament," *Dialogue: A Journal of Mormon Thought* 39, issue 2 (Summer 2006): 127-34.

How Frail a Foundation

Karen Rosenbaum

In 1963, at an informal dinner gathering of the Stanford creative writing program, I was sitting on a lawn chair on a patio in the Los Altos hills. One of my teachers, Richard Scowcroft, a former Utahn and a former Mormon, got down on his knees in front of me. "Are you really still a Mormon?" he asked, incredulous. "Why?"

I spluttered something that satisfied neither one of us. In the decades since then, I have been asked a version of that question countless times. Even more frequently I have asked it of myself.

When I was a teenager, belief came hard for me—and it has gotten progressively harder. I have never been able to say "this is true" about spiritual life in general or about Mormonism in particular. Despite decades of immersion in Mormonism, despite prayer and study, I feel I *know* almost nothing. Considering the tentative state of my testimony and considering the world in which I live—my husband and most of my associates are not believers—one is certainly justified in asking why it is I stay.

Shortly after critic and humorist Joe Queenan published a book called *True Believers* about the "religion" of sports, I heard him interviewed on National Public Radio. Queenan is from Philadelphia and has been an exasperated Phillies fan through 10,000 losses. How does he feel about his Phillies, asks the interviewer. "I have hated them since I was a little kid," says Queenan.

"Don't you secretly love them?" asks the interviewer.

"No," Queenan says. He admits he checks their scores every day—he says it's like making sure a relative is still breathing.

"Then why don't you divorce the Phillies?" asks the interviewer. "Become a Washington Senators or New York Yankees fan."

"Because," says Queenan, "people who switch allegiances go to hell. You have to play the cards you're dealt."

I know the Phillies aren't really comparable to Mormonism. Still, Queenan's relationship with the Phillies is a little bit like my relationship with the Church. Sometimes when I'm asked why I stay, I reply: "It's who I am." I was dealt a hand from a Mormon deck.

Someone, however, must have sneaked some other cards into my hand. Besides being a Mormon, I am also, from my core, a questioner, struggling with answers I have been given. Sometimes I am a searcher—seeking with great effort answers that work for me. I am often a coward—so I have not voiced my quandaries nor asked my questions very loudly. At times I am a sluggard. A friend who shares this torpor paraphrases Newton's first law of motion: a body will proceed the way it has been going unless rerouted by an outside power. Evidently, my friend continues to say, we stay in the Church because we haven't been acted upon by an influence that is strong enough to alter our course.

Both Mormon doctrine and humanistic philosophies say we can change. I can repent of pride and become more meek. I can repent of selfishness and become more altruistic. I shouldn't have to stay a frog; through my own efforts and through grace, I can be transformed into a princess—even though I have a lot more in common with frogs.

A few years ago, I heard a thoughtful sacrament service talk called "Why God?" in which the high councilman made a case for believing in God. He claimed we could *will* ourselves to make a leap of faith, bounding over troubling obstacles and concerns, to reach the hope of eternal life and eternal meaning.

Many of my friends have made the leap out of Mormonism—but I suspect I cannot change my Mormonness. As long as I have a mind, Mormon hymns will run through it. I cannot erase them—even those I don't like.

This is the kind of Mormon I am: I grew up in southern Nevada and northern Utah with a believing Mormon mother and an agnostic Jewish father who agreed their children would be raised in the LDS Church. (I am quite sure my dear father didn't know what he was agreeing to.) I have two brothers— one is a faithful Mormon; the other left the Church after high school. I love all my relatives, but because of age differences, personality traits, and geography, I am closer to the Jewish side of my family than to the Mormon side. I am married to a man who abandoned Mormonism in his twenties, a few years after he successfully completed a mission. I pay a tithe to the Church humanitarian fund. I have never requested my temple endowments. When I am home, I attend sacrament meeting and sometimes Sunday school, but not Relief Society and rarely stake meetings. I have said no to many Church callings that I felt I could not, in conscience, perform, but have had for many years a calling that no one else seems to want and that I enjoy—I produce the ward newsletter. When asked, I give talks, but not prayers, in Church.

Because I am what Jeff Burton and Juanita Brooks would probably call a Mormon on the edge, I am often ill at ease within the larger Church, but I'm fairly comfortable in my own ward. I have chosen carefully where I live and what ward I attend.

Gene England's inspired article, "The Church Is as True as the Gospel," didn't convert me to its thesis because I already felt the Church—at least my little part of it—was as true as, and maybe truer than, the gospel. In my ward, I haven't had to struggle much to practice Christian virtue. Gene would probably think I've made things too easy for myself.

The Berkeley ward is not the font of liberalism some might expect. In fact, another ward in our stake is more liberal. The high councilman who gave the "Why God" talk is from that ward. Most of the people in the Berkeley ward are more orthodox than I am. The ward comprises old folks, small and medium-sized families, single women and men, and a large contingent of young couples, many of them Cal graduate students, whose children fill up our Primary classes. We have functioning Young Women's and Young Men's programs. We—both men and women—are working and retired teachers, plumbers, salespersons, counselors, office workers, engineers, handymen, scientists, lawyers, business owners, computer programmers. We are, in approximately equal numbers, Democrats and Republicans. We are mostly Caucasian, but also Asian-American, Latino, and Black. Many of us spend a lot of time outside the tribe, affiliating with others with whom we share professions, causes, pastimes, or neighborhoods.

Usually I feel welcome at Church. Also welcome is my husband, who accompanies me to ward parties, especially dinners where there are vegetarian options—which is most of the parties in a ward situated in the middle of Berkeley's "Gourmet Ghetto." Berkeley warders whom we most admire include a senior couple (he in his nineties) who, after retirement, served two Peace Corps missions and now raise kiwis on top of their garage and sleep in a queen-sized bed on their patio. We also find stimulating the company of the younger members, including the temporary students. One favorite couple, though they have since moved to more secure academic jobs, was a mainstay in the ward: she was the gospel doctrine teacher, he was the chair of the activities committee. He, a non-member, used to say that he would like to join the Berkeley ward, but not the Mormon Church.

One of the best things for me about my association with Mormons, primarily the Mormons in my ward, is that some of them are not particularly literary or academic or sophisticated. They are not like the people with whom I ordinarily spend time—not like the people in our book group or birding group or my former teachers' group or swimming group or writing group, not like the folks in MoveOn.org. These "regular folks" aren't much like the Mormon people I enjoy most. I don't share a lot of my thoughts with them, but I listen to and try to learn from them. They afford me a less skewed view of the world than I would otherwise have. It's as hard for a Bay Area resident as it is for a Utahn to get a very accurate, unfiltered view of the world.

It isn't just the Berkeley ward that keeps me tethered to Mormonism. Although I have many good non-Mormon, non-Utah relatives and friends, many of my oldest and closest friends have at least some connection to Mormondom. They understand me in ways my un-Mormon friends (those without a Mormon connection) rarely can—even if they don't share my ambiguity toward the Church. These friends would not disown me were I to renounce Mormonism. They are part of my Mormon core.

Some of these friends I delight in seeing at Sunstone symposia. The publications and associations with *Sunstone* and *Dialogue* are two of the reasons I stay Mormon. Since 1962, four years before Gene co-founded *Dialogue*, I have been one of the lucky beneficiaries of friendship with the England family. They are among the friends who inspire me by their willingness to do what I'm not always able to do—really *embrace* Mormonism.

I am also close to many who have divorced Mormonism. But it is our Mormon past that binds us together, so their departure from the fold in an ironic way keeps me still attached to the Church.

The faith of some of them has been tried by historical dilemmas about the Book of Mormon, the lives and motives of Joseph Smith and Brigham Young, and more important, what would seem to be exclusion and limited compassion on the part of some current prophets and apostles. One advantage to having little faith is that there isn't much to shake. Perhaps I have been able—partly because I live a couple of states away—to separate myself from Salt Lake City and concern myself with what I call the really big questions.

For me the really big questions involve the existence and caring of heavenly parents and the legitimacy of my own thoughts and actions. What is truth? Is there divine guidance, and is it available to me? Am I doing what is worthwhile? Am I blessing others? Am I making the world a little bit better for those close to me and even those farther away? Because I am so busy dealing with these questions, I don't have as much space for the dilemmas that have occupied some of my friends.

When bad things happen to the faithful Mormon people whom I love, I am grateful for their faith and desperately want them to find comfort in it. Because I have less faith, I have less comfort. I want them not to lie awake at night as I do, worry as I do, feel uneasy and unsure as I do. I also don't want them to lie awake worrying about my soul, so I work hard to stay connected, however tenuously, to Mormonism.

And, finally, one more reason I stay connected. In the early part of "Why the Church Is as True as the Gospel," Gene

England tells of being a restless twelve-year-old in a stake conference—and suddenly, because he was *there*, he "became aware ... of the presence of the Holy Ghost and the special witness of Jesus Christ." Perhaps if I stay in the church, some day, because I am *there*, I will be touched in that way. Perhaps I will be able to brush off my warty little soul and *will* myself to leap to hope and eternal meaning.

My Leaps of Faith

Charlotte England

Growing up in Salt Lake City, my Church, community, and social life were very integrated. Our chapel was a turn-of-the-century building on Emerson Avenue below fifteenth east. Most of the time, we walked to Church for Sunday school in the morning and then later for sacrament meeting in the evening. We didn't mind the walk to Church since it was mostly down hill but weren't always happy with having to climb back up to our house afterward, especially in the summer. Occasionally, when my father hadn't taken the car to early morning priesthood meeting, we all piled into the Dodge and drove to Church. On Wednesdays we walked the six blocks from Uintah Elementary School for Primary.

By the time I was in high school, we had a new chapel just a block from our home. We all contributed to the ward budget and actively participated in building the chapel. Even we children played our part, helping with small jobs like clearing the field of weeds for planting grass, cleaning the building in preparation for its dedication, and giving our few cents toward the ward budget.

Ward dances were held almost weekly after MIA (Mutual Improvement Association) with Brother Condie furnishing ice cream from his shop. I remember reaching down into the big five-gallon containers to scoop one of our favorite flavors and getting a whiff of something that made me feel a little light-headed—peach brandy. To use Garrison Keillor's description, ours "was a community of good ordinary people who would give the shirt off their back if needed."

This was my community. It was there between home and Church that I learned my first gospel lessons and heard the warnings about choosing between right and wrong. I must have taken the lesson on faith quite literally because I tested it when I was about nine years old. I took an umbrella and climbed on top of our garage, opened the umbrella, grasped the handle, and made a big leap.

It was a hard landing. I came away slightly dazed and bruised but not broken. It was literally my first leap of faith and my first realization that a little more knowledge could have spared some bruises and a slightly wounded ego. Little did I know that my life would lead to unimagined adventures, some far beyond the safety and security of the Salt Lake Valley and that I would continue to be required to take leaps of faith.

Over the years I have had to make leaps of several kinds, much different from that of a little girl stepping off the roof with her umbrella. After I married Gene England in 1954, my horizons broadened enormously. With Gene, leaps were more like jumps out of an airplane—with a parachute! For instance, within a few months of being married, Gene and I were called to serve a mission to the Samoan Islands. We sold our car to help cover the forty-dollars-a-month cost for most of our mission. We filled two old trunks with everything we thought we would need for living and some teaching aids for the Samoan children.

A short time later, still newlyweds, we boarded the train at the Union Pacific Station in Salt Lake and waved goodbye to family and friends from the caboose. With us were fourteen other missionaries who were on their way to Australia and New Zealand. Before reaching our destination, we stopped in Hawaii for refueling and supplies and then landed in Suva, Fiji, for a ten-day wait for a freighter to Samoa. As we stood on the dock amid our trunks and suitcases, watching the ship pull away from the dock and leaving us in this strange new land, we looked around and wondered, "What now?"

After surviving what turned out to be a pleasant wait in Fiji, we experienced two rough days on a boat a fraction of the size of the one that had brought us to Fiji. When the boat came to rest on an early morning in the harbor of Apia on Upolu Island, we had our first glimpse of Samoa. We were a little intoxicated by the lush green foliage set off by flashing blue water. The mission president and his wife met us on deck and told us of our assignment, which was to teach school in Vaiola, a village on top of a volcanic mountain on the large primitive island of Savaii.

A few days later a small boat took us to Savaii, where some poorly nourished horses with saddle bags carried us from the coast to the top of the mountain and Vaiola. As we slowly rode up the hill into the dense forest and jungle heat, I felt like I was on another planet. The reality of it all was just beginning to sink in. Was it really faith that compelled me to jump from that garage or was it blind stupidity? It occurred to me that I could use a larger umbrella for the leap we were now about to take. The horse plodded along with a rhythm matching the rhythm of my thoughts as I told myself, "I can do this. I can do this," not knowing exactly just what "it" was other than learning Samoan and teaching and working with people in the village.

We arrived at the old run-down house built near the turn of the century that we lived in, along with three "cowboy elders" who ran the coconut plantation and tractors and a

The road to Vaiola was just a dirt path in 1954. Even with the improvements shown here, it remained a road less traveled. The elementary school survived to be joined by a small Church college with a combined enrollment of a few hundred students. Photograph ca. 1992 by Dennis Marsico. © Corbis Images fourth elder who was the school principal. Gene and I would occupy the home with them for the next six months. We had no electricity, and our water came from a barrel that collected rainwater from our roof. During the following weeks and months, my silent mantra was, "I can do this. I really can do this."

We settled into our teaching routine, worked with the branch members, and visited people in an even more quaint nearby village where swallows swooped down around the *fales,* or Samoan houses, at dusk. It created a most peaceful setting that I am always reminded of when I see swallows at sunset.

We studied the language each morning, combining it with our scripture study by translating the Pearl of Great Price from English to Samoan. We scrubbed our clothes on a wash board and draped them over the bushes to dry. Gene fashioned an ironing board out of a piece of wood and then, as I ironed on one end with a kerosene-powered iron, he anchored the other while reading to me. Thus, he got a freshly-ironed shirt while I got to hear poetry, wisdom from Lowell Bennion, or the Pogo comic strip.

We also managed a make-shift first aid station using the few resources we had to bandage and disinfect boils and minor wounds or larger ones from encounters with wild boar. Constantly, there were new challenges that kept us mindful of why we were there and pushed us to find creative ways that worked for the benefit of the Samoan people, whom we had come to cherish.

A couple of months into our teaching, Gene contracted a rash on his hand, possibly an allergic reaction to the chalk we used at school. I tried to clear it up with the remedies we had, but what seemed a simple irritation soon developed into a serious infection. When small blisters formed, I bathed his hand in a solution that I hoped would keep the infection from spreading. One morning when he didn't feel up to teaching and I was changing the dressing before leaving to take care of our classes, I turned his hand over to find two red veins going up his arm to the lymph nodes, indicating that he had blood poisoning. Realizing the seriousness of his illness, I said to myself, "This can't be. Not here. Not now. So far away from a doctor and a hospital." The sunny world we were still adjusting to suddenly turned dark and overwhelming. Everything— the decaying house, the lush jungle, the village, the people— was suddenly foreign to me. I asked myself, "What are we doing here?" I was looking for direction, perhaps a voice to tell me what I could do to make it all better. I begged, "Please dear God, please don't leave us here alone."

Fasting and prayer took on a much greater significance over the next three days as I somehow found the strength to take care of everything that needed attention, to be with Gene every spare moment, hoping and praying for a miracle, and to also fill in at the school and fulfill our obligations to other people. I drew on all the resources available. The gruff-speaking cowboy elders and principal gave Gene a blessing. A woman in the village who was considered a healer came to offer help. By the third day, I woke up after having fallen asleep by Gene's side and saw that the treacherous red lines had faded. I realized Gene would live. It was like a brilliant light shining into a dark space and I felt my burden lifted. My tears were joyous and probably a little hysterical, but I made no apologies. We were reminded of this experience for many years afterward. As Gene reported, "About twice a year (at no regular times) for the forty-five years since then, my finger has developed tiny, irritating sores, and I remember the wound and the healing."

Our lives followed a pretty routine path for a few years after our mission because we moved several times for military service, school, and jobs, finishing degrees and having six children along the way. We also renovated an old Victorian house in Palo Alto that we were content to stay in for the rest of our lives. We had close friends there who were like family to us. Their children and ours grew up together like cousins. It was a good place to be and there were lots of reasons to stay, mostly for the community of friends and the support we felt there.

We took another leap of faith when, along with a small group of dedicated friends, we helped launch *Dialogue: A Journal of Mormon Thought.* We soon found that many of our fellow Saints were hungry for intellectual discussion of gospel subjects. One early reader wrote, "Reading *Dialogue* was like finding water in the desert." We even had the support and participation of some general authorities as well as our stake president and mayor of Palo Alto, the future apostle David B. Haight, who saw the need for the journal and encouraged our efforts.

Support increased as Gene responded to invitations to speak about the journal to groups in the bay area. The audiences were a mix of subscribers and readers and some who were just curious to see what kind of creature the man might be who was behind such a venture. Some came prepared to attack the journal and the person responsible for it. Generally, it didn't take long for people to realize that Gene was a faithful Latter-day Saint, not a wild-eyed radical, as some people supposed, out to undermine the Church.

Our life in Palo Alto ended with a phone call from a former colleague of Gene's inviting him to teach at St. Olaf's Lutheran College in Northfield, Minnesota. This was another big leap, but different from that first one we had taken sixteen years earlier as two young twenty-year-olds in Samoa. This time there was more conviction to the words still sounding in my head, "We can do it. We really can." With help from friends, we packed, rented a U-Haul truck, and said goodbye to the old Victorian house we had put so much of our lives into. Gene turned *Dialogue* over to the capable hands of Bob Rees, and we headed for Minnesota.

We moved into a faculty house near the college and were still unpacking when I received a call from the mission president's wife in Minneapolis. (You've got to say one thing for the Church, they know how to find you!) She asked me to do something that was far beyond my experience, which often happens in the Church. A recently deceased elderly sister, after living severely crippled and bed-ridden for years in the Odd Fellows Home in Northfield, had made a request that she be buried in her temple clothing. The mission president's wife asked me to attend to the matter and dress the body. I suppressed my urge to say, "You've got to be kidding."

Instead, I suggested that there must be someone who did this sort of thing better than I could and who would be more comfortable doing it. I couldn't manage the words to express my own fear of death. She made it clear that I was that someone and suggested I bring one of the other three sisters from our little branch to help since that would give them an opportunity to serve as well. I called each sister and each refused. A little later, one of them, Jean Jacobsen, called back to say she would do it.

We were both a little frightened as we approached the room where the body lay on a table covered with plastic. After a prayer asking for support in this ritual that was far beyond the realm of our experience, we carefully started dressing the small body and, as we did, tried to imagine what her life might have been like before she was no longer able to care for herself and had to depend on others. We imagined her with little children, cooking meals, caring for her home and family. By the time we finished, my fear of death was gone and I felt a kinship with this woman whom I had never met in life. Dressing the body with my new friend Jean created a bond that has lasted these many years.

This was another jumping-off experience for me. I again learned the strength that is found by taking on a request that can be frightening. When we're asked to serve, we don't always get to choose our calling or the people with whom we work, but the sweet surprise comes when friendships develop with persons I may not have chosen from the crowd.

At times the very community in which I find support and strength challenges my faith to the degree that I'm tempted to shut down and not ask hard questions. I see life as one long conversation in which we are responsible for the degree of engagement we choose. I figure this life is a continuation of our experiences in our pre-mortal life. We come to this life with gifts and talents we are charged by God to employ as we continue to discuss with ourselves and others what we will do and why. I think it is important to include other people in our conversations, to listen to what they say in a caring and non-judgmental way, and to appreciate the contributions they make to our communities, utilizing the gifts that God gave them.

During a conversation about a topic that required more than a pat answer, a friend once remarked to me, "A troubled belief is not the same as disbelief." Her words comforted me at the time and have many times since when my personal beliefs have taken a beating and I have been unable to find the peace I had experienced in Samoa and Northfield. I have always operated on the assumption that intelligent people can discuss anything of consequence by seeking clarity and understanding and finding mutual acceptance even if they don't agree.

Gene and I found our faith challenged later in our lives by the behavior of people in positions of power in the Church. I saw a contradiction between their behavior and the principles they espoused, and their actions directly affected us and our family. During some of these trying times, friends and associates wondered why we didn't jump ship. While I understood why they would think that, for us, such an action would mean abandoning our core beliefs, which were too deeply embedded for us to forsake.

The most profound crisis of faith I have faced in my life, the one that caused me to examine where I stood on the question of staying or leaving, came during Gene's illness and death. The night I took him to the emergency room, I sat by his hospital bed waiting for my children to gather, pleading with God as I had forty-eight years earlier in the jungles of Samoa, asking once again for a miracle. The difference was that now we were in a hospital with skilled physicians and all the advantages of modern medicine. As I looked around, I wondered, "How does faith work with all this knowledge and technology?"

I regret that I didn't think to save a lock of Gene's hair when I kissed him before they wheeled him into surgery. Radiation erased the little bit of hair that was left after surgery. Throughout our married life, whenever we traveled, I loved reaching over to brush my hand through his thick brown hair. Such a small pleasure among so many of the little things between us that I miss these days.

Priesthood holders gave Gene blessings that were full of promises. The bishop told me after his blessing that he felt sure that Gene would recover and do his greatest writing. I desperately wanted to believe him and pinned my faith on his and others' words. I marveled at the devotion of our children, each with his or her particular gift of tender care for their father. To the very end, we hoped for a miracle. When Gene died, the world felt alien to me and I could not find a place in it. I was fortunate not to be given the usual clichéd reasons for Gene's death. For me, there was only one explanation: he had acquired a hideously aggressive tumor that grew faster than it could be cured.

Because of that experience, I see God as a being who is nearby and knows and understands our grief. I imagine that He is pleased when we exercise faith and choose to face our trials and learn from them, just as when we watch our own children find their way, making choices that are sometimes painful to us but yet grateful they keep trying after they stumble.

How can I say that I'm grateful for these experiences when I miss Gene so much, when I no longer have his hand to hold, and when I have to take yet another leap of faith in order not to waver? I am consoled by a feeling that he still tries to reach out to me, to take a leap of faith right along with me. One such incident occurred about three months after he died when I got a call from a woman named Phyllis asking me to teach a class on art appreciation at Elderquest, an extension of UVSC. I turned her down. She called again and I explained that I wasn't fit to teach anybody because I couldn't concentrate or even care to make the effort to think about anything of consequence.

She didn't give up. Neither did my children, once they learned of her invitation. Between pressure from Phyllis, who I later learned was a grief counselor, and my children, I finally gave in and took the job. I dug out my old art history notes, pictures, and anything that would help the class understand and appreciate works of art. Through this and other experiences, gradually I was able to work my way out of the deep, dark hole I was in after losing Gene and start creating the new life that I would live without my dear Gene.

I will never forget the morning of my first class as I carried my heavy folder with lecture notes and illustrations through the senior center to the room assigned to me. As I took a deep breath and told myself, "This is it! You're on, kiddo!" I felt, just before entering the room full of people, that a rather firm but gentle shove from behind pushed me across the threshold. I think Gene was there, helping me take my next big leap of faith.

I Place It in My Heart

Robert A. Rees

> The gospel is true, is true.
> Everything else is anybody's guess.
> —Robert A. Christmas[1]

Over the course of a lifetime, I have had occasion to give thought to the question of why I continue to be an active, committed member of the Church of Jesus Christ of Latter-day Saints. The question has seemed more poignant during periods when official actions of the Church have clashed with my own expectations of how the Church should respond, including during the Civil Rights Movement and the denial of the priesthood to blacks, the battle over the Equal Rights Amendment, and over the past several decades, the Church's treatment of homosexuals. The question of staying has also been raised at times when I have experienced deep pain over the way I and others have been treated by ecclesiastical leaders.

Up to this point—and I suspect this will hold true for the remainder of my life—my strategy has been to deal quietly and privately with personal pain and try to work for change on important issues from within the Church. I realize that this is not the only possible strategy, but it is the one I have chosen. The reasons I choose to stay fall into the following categories: people, principles, and commitments.

People

One of the chief reasons I stay is related to others, including my family of origin, my siblings, my wife's family, my children and grandchildren, friends, and people with whom I have a tangential relationship but whose faith is somehow connected to mine. I also stay in the hope that my staying may have an influence on future generations.

My family converted to the Restored Gospel in four separate generations beginning with my great-great-grandparents in Wales in the first great missionary gathering there. They and their three sons immigrated to the Great Basin in the 1850s, although the parents and one son returned to Wales shortly thereafter. Another son stayed in Utah where he became a prominent educator; the third son, my great-grandfather, David Rees, moved to Missouri and joined the Reorganized Church. My grandfather, Zoram Rees, although bearing a Book of Mormon name, never belonged to the Church. His wife, my grandmother Emma Jane Maddox Rees, was converted by Mormon missionaries traveling through southwestern Colorado during the 1920s. Two of my aunts were also baptized at this time, but my father, then a boy of twelve, was not. However, when he was in his twenties, he became converted through what he considered a miraculous priesthood healing. This occurred when I was a young boy and he and my mother had been divorced for some time.

When I was ten, my father returned from World War II to tell me about the gospel and baptize me in the Mesa Temple. Thus, there have been four independent conversions of my family over five generations. It is therefore partly because of what I consider the Lord's persistence with the Rees family, and out of respect for the sacrifices my forebears made in sustaining it, that I remain committed to the Lord's great latter-day work.

In spite of these various conversions, there was a period of many years when I was the only member of my family active in the Church. I remember many Sunday mornings during my teenage years when I rode the bus alone to the Long Beach First Ward and later to the Long Beach Fifth Ward. I believe that my faithfulness during those and subsequent years may have influenced my father and several siblings in eventually returning to the Church. I am aware of how much happier my family has been because of their association with the Church. I stay because at times, in my family and my wife's family, there is no one else on hand to perform baptisms, give blessings, speak at funerals, and go to the temple with someone going for the first time—acts that I am happy to perform.

One of the most important reasons for my continued commitment is my hope for the future for my own children and grandchildren, some of whom are presently active in the Church and some of whom are not. I want them to know that the gospel has been the most powerful influence in shaping my life, including my role as father and grandfather. I hope that when they think of me, they can say, as e. e. cummings said of his father,

> because my Father lived his soul
> love is the whole and more than all.[2]

I stay for all of those to whom over the course of a lifetime I have taught the gospel and to whom I have borne personal witness as to the transforming power of the gospel and its particular expression within the Mormon faith. I still keep in touch with people I had the privilege of teaching the gospel to when I was a young missionary. Several years ago my former companions and I had a reunion with a group of converts from Kankakee, Illinois. It was a joyful occasion to see how profoundly the lives of the people we had brought to the Church had been affected by their decision to embrace the gospel. I also have a continuing relationship with many of the young adults to whom I ministered as a bishop of a singles' ward and also the good people of the Baltic States Mission my wife and I had the blessing of welcoming into the Church during the three and a half years we lived there. Witnessing the transformation of their lives through the Restored Gospel has been one of the most meaningful experiences of my life. It is among the Mormons that I have formed my deepest, most meaningful and most affectionate associations. I truly understand what it is to be liked and loved as a friend, to have bonds with men and women I believe will continue into the eternities.

I stay because of those I have met throughout my travels and in the various wards in which we have lived who feel estranged, who are different, whose ties to the Church are tenuous, who question and doubt. As I said to Karl Keller many years ago, "If all of those of us who see what is wrong with the Church leave, where will the Church's conscience be?"[3] I don't flatter myself that I am the Church's conscience, but I believe that, along with hundreds of thousands of others, I am part of that conscience.

Principles

Over the course of a lifetime, I have found the principles of the gospel to be enlightening, liberating, and ennobling. I speak of the first principles of faith and repentance as well as others we are more likely to neglect, such as those William Faulkner spoke of in his Nobel Prize acceptance speech:

"love and honor and pity and pride and compassion and sacrifice." Faulkner called these "eternal verities" because they deal with "the problems of the human heart in conflict with itself."[4] To Faulkner's list, I would add courage, humility, and integrity. I believe the Church is a laboratory in which these principles can be acted upon. It isn't the only place, but it is one of the ideal places to do so.

More specifically, the Church gives us opportunities to go outside and beyond ourselves in ways that school our souls and enlarge our hearts. These include small sacrifices such as fasting, paying tithes and offerings, and serving others. Were it not for the Church's encouragement to spend one day a month going without food or drink, I doubt I would hold in my heart an understanding of the privation millions throughout the world endure daily or that I would contribute as regularly, however modestly, to relieve their suffering. Were it not for the Church, I would probably not contribute a tenth of my income to charity. Nor would I be as likely to put aside personal comforts and desires in order to serve others. Ironically, these small sacrifices have deepened and enriched my life immeasurably.

Among the principles the Church has taught me to follow, even though it has not always been happy with how I have done so, is the moral imperative to work for social justice and to respectfully challenge and question the Church itself when, in my judgment, it has fallen short of its own stated ideals. It has taught me to minister to those whom society considers "the least" among us, those whom Mother Teresa called "Jesus in disguise."

The Church affords me numerous opportunities to live the Golden Rule, to do unto others as I would have them do unto me. I believe this principle applies to the institution of the Church itself—that we are obligated to do unto it as we would have it do unto us, which is a reason I continue to give it my allegiance in spite of the fact that I sometimes feel it is not always completely deserving of it. I believe a higher manifestation of this principle, as it applies both to individuals and to institutions, is to not do unto others as they have done unto us.[5] Acting on this principle requires even greater courage, humility, and love.

The principles I mention are best exemplified in the life of Christ and best followed within a community where people can work together to give them concrete manifestation. I stay because these principles produce goodness, and I want to be a part of that goodness, to help magnify it in the world.

Commitments

One of the reasons I stay is because of promises and covenants I have made to the Lord and to others to remain faithful. When I was a boy of fifteen, I traveled from our small Arizona town to Mesa to receive my patriarchal blessing. Alma Davis, the patriarch who laid his hands on my head that day, made what I consider inspired and wonderful promises which began to unfold in my life through serious, sustained engagement within the Church. Patriarch Davis spoke of covenants I had made in the preexistence, including the reciprocal promise that I would have God's Spirit "as a guide and companion." Although I can't say I have always been worthy of it, I have felt the guidance and companionship of that Spirit at critical times in my life.

Every Sunday I renew my covenant with Christ when, to use Bruce Jorgensen's image, I take the sacramental "thimble / of water and shard of bread."[6] That weekly renewal of my bond is one of the most meaningful rituals in my life. It keeps fresh in my mind and my imagination the reality of Christ's mercy and unconditional love. It keeps fresh my promise to remember that I have taken upon myself his name and all that this implies of lifting the burdens and binding the wounds of others.

Similarly, fifty years ago my wife and I covenanted with each other across the altar of the temple. The connection between us has only deepened and expanded over the years. Part of that covenant included the stewardship we share for the spiritual welfare of our children. We find hope in what the prophet Joseph Smith said about "eternal sealings of faithful parents" whose faithfulness would "save not only themselves, but likewise their posterity," the "careless and disobedient" among their offspring who had wandered from the Church.[7] Or as Brigham Young put it, "I care not where those children go, they are bound up to their parents by an everlasting tie, and no power on earth or hell can separate them from their parents in eternity."[8] Considering the principle of agency, on one level, this promise does not make sense to me, but on another, like the speaker in Thomas Hardy's poem, "The Oxen," who though doubting a folk tale about oxen kneeling at Christ's birth, nevertheless goes to his own barn on Christmas Eve, "hoping it might be so."[9]

Additional reasons

Beyond those mentioned above, I stay in the Church because I want to be part of the spiritual and social revolution that began when Joseph Smith knelt in the grove of trees near Palmyra. For all the limitations of the Church itself, over a lifetime of the study of religion I find Mormonism the most satisfying and enlightening religious philosophy of all. The concept of a godhood consisting of a personal, loving Heavenly Father and Heavenly Mother, the parents of fallible but perfectible children, is extremely appealing and deeply soul-satisfying. In fact, I find Mormon doctrines to be among the most enlightened in history. Consider, for example, the teachings embedded in Joseph Smith's King Follett Discourse and Section 84 of the Doctrine and Covenants that God desires to give his children everything he has: all knowledge, all power, all glory, even the ultimate and crowning glory of godhood itself. Is there a grander teaching in the annals of religion?

I stay because I love to sing Mormon hymns. Joining my voice with others on Sundays is a spiritual, kinesthetic experience. The songs of redeeming love, as Alma calls them, vibrate throughout our whole bodies and souls as we give full-hearted and full-throated expression to our feelings of praise and thanksgiving. One of the functions of hymn singing is to unify a congregation in a way that transcends their differences. For those few moments when we join our voices, expressing whatever we may feel of joy or gratitude, we are as one—even when we are not in complete harmony! In this way we "serve the Lord with gladness: com[ing] into his presence with singing" (Ps. 100:2).

I sincerely believe the Lord wants his Church to be better than it is, and I have the hope that I may play some small part in making it so. I believe he is not pleased when Church members see blacks, homosexuals, intellectuals, or anyone whom the majority consider "other" as unworthy to sit at his table. I don't believe God is pleased when dissent and open dialogue are discouraged, quashed, or especially punished. I don't believe he is pleased when women are relegated to second-class citizenship. I don't believe he looks kindly on our abandonment of gospel principles in support of partisan political positions.

I stay because I believe the Lord wants the Church to be more liberal. As Joseph Smith said, "Our Heavenly Father is more liberal in his views and more boundless in his mercies than we are ready to believe."[10] I applaud the emphasis on conservative spiritual and moral values, but I want us to emphasize as well the gospel's liberal social and political messages of equality and peace. The extent to which Church leaders and members counter corrosive moral decay is, to my mind, important in creating a world where God's children have sufficient opportunities to make good choices and find true happiness. On the other hand, the extent to which Church leaders and members work against important social and political reforms significantly hampers such goals. My belief is that the Lord will judge us unfavorably if we back politicians who fail to help the disadvantaged and powerless; who support unjust wars and the annihilation of innocent men, women, and children; who condone torture and other forms of inhumane treatment; and who degrade the environment we are charged to protect.

As my spiritual life has evolved, I have found myself certain of fewer things. In *The Great Gatsby*, F. Scott Fitzgerald's idealistic central character holds in his mind a fantastic image of Daisy Fay, a woman whom he has idealized. After Gatsby's dreams come in contact with the reality of who Daisy really is, we are told that "his count of enchanted objects had diminished by one."[11] In the face of historical revelations, scientific discoveries, and my own experience, the enchanted objects that hold my wonder have diminished; at the same time, the things I hold as pearls of great price have increased in value and certainty. William Sloane Coffin puts it perfectly: "[There] are those who prefer certainty to truth, those in church who put the purity of dogma ahead of the integrity of love. And what a distortion of the gospel it is to have limited sympathies and unlimited certainties, when the very reverse, to have limited certainties but unlimited sympathies, is not only more tolerant but far more Christian."[12]

Over the course of my life, I have had sacred experiences, occasions when "[my] heart burn[ed] within [me]" (Luke 24:32) that revealed or confirmed some essential truth or direction. Some may consider such experiences sentimental or self-deceiving, but as much as I can summon of intellectual and emotional honesty tells me they are valid experiences. They are one of the reasons I believe, in the sense of the Latin word for "I believe," *credo*, which is literally "I place it in my heart." That is what I have done with the Church's teachings when attended by spiritual confirmation.

The validity of such experiences and their positive effect on my devotion to the gospel and my commitment to the Church have put me in an uncomfortable place when I have felt compelled to address sensitive issues through my speaking and writing. To me, such expressions are a sign of my devotion, while to some others they are considered a sign of rebellion or even apostasy. To care enough to risk disapproval and punishment is to risk rejection and loneliness. The fact is, the Church is not a particularly friendly or hospitable place for people who have doubts or questions or who risk speaking out on moral issues. It is a difficult balancing act to follow when appropriate and disagree when conscience dictates. My sentiments during periods of stress are akin to those expressed by Robert Frost in his poem "Birches":

> It's when I'm weary of considerations,
> And life is too much like a pathless wood ... [that]
> I'd like to get away from earth awhile
> And then come back to it and begin over.

Frost adds:

> May no fate willfully misunderstand me
> And half grant what I wish and snatch me away
> Not to return. Earth's the right place for love.
> I don't know where it's likely to go better.[13]

At times I have had the impulse to get away from the Church

for "awhile / and then come back and begin over." Neverthe-less, I believe the Church is the right place, or at least one of the right places, for love. I don't know where it's likely to go better.

The ultimate reason I stay in the Mormon Church is because I have made a commitment to follow Christ. I believe the Church is one of the places in which his work is to be done. It is not the only place, but it is the one I have chosen—or perhaps that has chosen me. Because I know in the deep-est part of my being that Jesus loves me, that he suffered for my sins in Gethsemane and on Calvary, and still suffers when I fall short of my commitment to him, in my small and inad-equate way I am committed to following him. Christ calls us from the things of this world, and he calls us to his great work of bringing to pass the redemption of the world. Without our participation, that work cannot have its ultimate flowering. As Rumi says,

> Where Jesus lives, the great-hearted gather.
> We are a door that is never locked.
> If you suffer any kind of pain,
> Stay near this door. Open it.[14]

The saddest episode in scripture is that found in the Gospel of John where Christ, at the moment his disciples begin to abandon him, asks his chosen twelve, "Wilt thou also go away?" Peter's response is one that I have thought of when asked why I stay in the Church: "Lord, to whom shall we go? Thou hast the words of eternal life" (John 6:68). Jogging on the streets of Salt Lake City during a recent visit, I noticed that someone had stenciled on sidewalks through-out the downtown area the words, "Trust Jesus." I do trust him—I trust him to be fair, to be constant, to be loving.

A few weeks ago we celebrated Pioneer Day to honor

the sacrifices of the Mormon pioneers. There is an episode in their crossing this great land that is worth recounting. At Winter Quarters a serious discussion was held about whether to cross the plains late in the season with handcarts that had been hastily constructed out of unseasoned wood. Levi Savage argued in vain that the crossing was ill advised and likely to be disastrous. One of the apostles promised that if the Saints pressed on, they would transverse the wilderness without harm or loss of life. Savage knew better. "The tears rolled down his cheeks as he prophesied that if ... [they] took the journey at that late season of the year, their bones would strew the way." Nevertheless, he added, "If you elect to go ahead, I will come and assist, though it cost me my life."[15] They went, with Levi Savage accompanying them, and although, as he had predicted, many perished, he was instrumental in saving the lives of many. I don't consider myself to have the foresight or courage of Levi Savage, but his impulse to accompany the Saints on their journey, no matter how long or perilous, no matter how personally challenging, no matter the sacrifice or ultimate cost, is my impulse as well. Perhaps more than anything, it explains why I stay.

Notes

1. Robert A. Christmas, "Hungry Sunday," *Sunstone*, Apr. 1986, 23.

2. E. E. Cummings, "my father lived through dooms of love," online at *American Poems*, www.americanpoems.com.

3. Karl Keller and Robert A. Rees, "Letters of Belief: An Exchange of Thoughts and Feelings about the Mormon Faith," *Dialogue: A Journal of Mormon Thought* 9, no. 3 (Fall 1974): 9–20.

4. See "The Nobel Prize in Literature 1949: William Faulkner, Banquet Speech," City Hall, Stockholm, Dec. 10, 1950, online at the *Official Web Site of the Nobel Prize,* nobelprize.org.

5. As expressed by the feminist movement in Norway, "Do not do to them what they did to us," qtd. in William Sloane Coffin, "Liberty to the Captives and Good Things to the Afflicted," *Homosexuality and Christian Faith: Questions of Conscience for the Churches,* ed. Walter Wink (Minneapolis: Fortress Press, 1999), 109.

6. Bruce W. Jorgensen, "On Second West in Cedar City, Utah: Canticle for the Virgin," *Dialogue: A Journal of Mormon Thought* 6, no. 1 (Spring 1971): 65.

7. Orson F. Whitney, *Conference Report,* Apr. 1929, 110, qtd. in "Hope for Parents of Wayward Children," *Ensign,* Sept. 2002, 11.

8. Brigham Young, a sermon delivered Apr. 29, 1866, in *Journal of Discourses,* 26 vols. (Liverpool and London: Franklin D. Richards and the Latter-day Saints Book Depot), 11:215; qtd. in Joseph Fielding Smith, *Doctrines of Salvation,* comp. Bruce R. McConkie, 3 vols. (Salt Lake City: Deseret Book, 1954-56), 2:90-91.

9. Thomas Hardy, "The Oxen," available online at "The Oxen: A Poem for Christmas, 1915," *The Victorian Web: Literature, History, & Culture in the Age of Victoria,* www.victorianweb.org/authors/hardy/religionov.html.

10. Joseph Fielding Smith, comp. and ed., *Teachings of the Prophet Joseph Smith* (1938; Salt Lake City: Deseret Book, 1976), 256.

11. F. Scott Fitzgerald, *The Great Gatsby* (New York: Scribners, 1953), 94.

12. Coffin, "Liberty to the Captives," 106–07.

13. Robert Frost, "Birches," *The Poetry of Robert Frost: The Collected Poems, Complete and Unabridged,* ed. Henry Connery Lathem (New York: Holt, Rinehart, and Winston, 1964), 153.

14. Coleman Barks, transl., *The Essential Rumi* (Edison, NJ: Castle Books, 1995), 201.

15. Quoted in William L. Knecht, "A Lesson from the Past," *Dialogue: A Journal of Mormon Thought* 5, no. 3 (Fall 1970): 80.

About the Contributors

Lavina Fielding Anderson (Ph.D., English, University of Washington) is a past president of the Association for Mormon Letters, former editor of the *Journal of Mormon History,* and past associate editor of *Dialogue: A Journal of Mormon Thought.* She is a recipient of the Grace Fort Arrington Award for Distinguished Service from the Mormon History Association. She is the editor of *Lucy's Book: A Critical Edition of Lucy Mack Smith's Family Memoir* and co-editor of *Chesterfield: Mormon Outpost in Idaho, Sisters in Spirit: Mormon Women in Historical and Cultural Perspective,* and *Tending the Garden: Essays on Mormon Literature.* She is a contributor to four anthologies, including *On Their Own: Widows and Widowhood in the American Southwest, 1848-1939.*

Molly McLellan Bennion is a Seattle attorney who has practiced law since 1984. She studied government at Smith College and history and education at the University of Washington before entering the University of Houston Law Center, where she became a member of the *Law Review* staff her first year. She has served on the board of directors of *Dialogue: A Journal of Mormon Thought* for twelve years, twice as chair, and published articles in *Dialogue, Sunstone,* and other LDS publications. As a teenager she was named Spokane Lilac Queen and thereafter spent a year addressing civic groups about the economic advantages of Eastern Washington. She says her life has been filled with "the usual kinds of things people do who must be flexible for family reasons when they have four children and aging parents but who are altogether too type-A."

Mary Lythgoe Bradford has taught English at Brigham Young University and the University of Utah. For fifteen years she was a writing consultant for the U.S. General Accounting Office in Washington, D.C. She is the author of *Leaving Home: Personal Essays* (Award for Best Personal Essays, Association for Mormon Letters), *Lowell L. Bennion: Teacher, Counselor, Humanitarian* (Evans Biography Award, Mountain West Center for Regional Studies; Ella Larsen Turner Best Biography Award, Mormon History Association), and *Purple: Poems*. She is a past editor of *Dialogue: A Journal of Mormon Thought*. She is the editor of two anthologies, *Mormon Women Speak* and *Personal Voices: A Celebration of Dialogue*. She says she hopes to live long enough to finish her autobiography.

William S. Bradshaw is Professor Emeritus of Molecular Biology at Brigham Young University where he received the Karl G. Maeser Distinguished Teaching Award and other honors. He is co-author of *Biological Science: A Molecular Approach* and *Guidance for LDS Families with LGBT Children*, as well as a contributor to the *Encyclopedia of Mormonism*. He has published in *Dialogue: A Journal of Mormon Thought* and *Sunstone* magazine and in professional publications such as *Cell Biology Education–Life Sciences Education* and *Journal of Biochemical Toxicology*. With his wife, Marge, he presided over the Hong Kong and South Vietnam Mission from 1971 to 1974. They are currently co-chairs of Family Fellowship, a support group for LDS parents of gay and lesbian children.

D. Jeff Burton is a mechanical engineer (MS, University of Michigan) and past president of the American Industrial Hygiene Association. Although in private practice, he has been a lecturer at the University of California Berkeley and College of Medicine at the University of Utah. He is the author of some fourteen monographs on industrial hygiene and ventilation systems. In the area of religion, he is the author of *For Those Who Wonder,* a book exploring LDS cultural approaches to faith; a forthcoming novel, *Eternal Borderlands;* and a regular column in *Sunstone* magazine. He has served two LDS missions, one in his youth to Japan and one more recently to LDS Church headquarters in downtown Salt Lake City.

Claudia L. Bushman is a former Professor of American Studies at Columbia University and founding editor of the Mormon feminist publication *Exponent II.* In recent years, she and her husband blazed a new trail in LDS scholarship as they established the curriculum for Mormon Studies at Claremont Graduate University in Southern California. She has published twelve books of social and cultural history and Mormonism, including *Building the Kingdom: A History of Mormons in America, Contemporary Mormonism: Latter-day Saints in Modern America,* and *Mormon Sisters: Women in Early Utah.* Her twelfth book is *Pansy's Family History: Margaret E. P. Gordon, 1866-1966,* an edited autobiography of her maternal grandmother. She was named New York State's Mother of the Year in 2002.

Fred Christensen is a retired neurosurgeon living in Arizona. He is the author of an autobiographical sketch, *Stopping the Pain,* that relates unusual medical experiences and the rationale of faith as important in the life of a medical professional. A lifelong Latter-day Saint, he is a descendant of John Pack, one of the original scouts to enter the Salt Lake Valley ahead of Brigham Young. As a young man, Christensen served as a captain at Travis Air Force Base in California for two years. In retirement he organized the Navajo Volunteer Literary Program to manage and train seventy-five volunteers who tutor children at a Title One school in Scottsdale. For this he has received the prestigious Hon Kachina ("healing spirit") Award for community service.

Charlotte England is a watercolor artist, teacher, and humanitarian living in Provo. As a young woman, she studied music and art at the University of Utah, Brigham Young University, and St. Olaf College, including an interim class in France to study and perform with the St. Olaf Chamber Ensemble. She has served on the Sunstone Foundation board and currently heads the Eugene and Charlotte England Foundation which sponsors writing contests, humanities research, and scholarships. She has regularly opened her home for recitals, literary readings for the Association for Mormon Letters, disaster-relief drives, and environmental projects. She is also known to BYU students as the one-time proprietor of Charlotte's Original Ice Cream in downtown Provo.

When **Lael Littke** was an Idaho farm girl, she dreamed of being a writer, living in New York City, and dating Cary Grant. She achieved two of those dreams (Cary Grant eluded her). She has had over forty young adult and children's books published. She has also collaborated on three women's novels and achieved one on her own in 2011, *Keepers of Blackbird Hill*. Four of her books were featured on the New York Public Library's "Recommended List for Teenagers," *Blue Skye* received a Notable Work of Fiction Award from the Southern California Council on Children's Literature, and *Prom Dress* received the flattering, if also dubious, honor of being named "the book most often stolen" at one school library. She has taught writing classes at Pasadena City College and UCLA.

Armand L. Mauss is author of three books on Mormon history and culture: *All Abraham's Children: Changing Mormon Conceptions of Race and Lineage, The Angel and the Beehive: The Mormon Struggle for Assimilation,* and (with Lester E. Bush) *Neither White nor Black: Mormon Scholars Encounter the Race Issue in a Universal Church,* as well as other academic books, including *Social Problems as Social Movements.* An Emeritus Professor of Sociology and Religious Studies at Washington State University, he has recently taught courses in Mormon Studies at Claremont Graduate University. He is a past editor of the *Journal for the Scientific Study of Religion* and past president of the Mormon History Association.

Chase N. Peterson received his A.B. and M.D. from Harvard University. After a fellowship at Yale, he entered private practice in internal medicine and later returned to Harvard as Dean of Admissions and Vice President of Alumni Affairs and Development. Back in Utah, he became Vice President of Health Sciences at the University of Utah and later president of the university. For the last ten years, he has been a Professor of Family Medicine and co-director of the third-year family medicine clerkships at the university medical school. He is also a board member with the Utah Symphony Orchestra and a member of the Utah Citizens' Counsel, an advocacy group that opposes gerrymandering.

Grethe B. Peterson received her B.A. from Brigham Young University and studied at Radcliffe College, Southern Connecticut College, Harvard University, and the University of Utah. She was a member of the original *Exponent II* staff, chaired the Utah Endowment for the Humanities, founded Women Concerned about Nuclear War, and was a member of the LDS Young Women's General Board and the Salt Lake Olympic Committee. As a member of the Utah State Task

Force on Sexual Abuse, she was insrumental in creating the Children's Justice Centers, of which there are now seventeen throughout the state of Utah. The centers facilitate investigation and prosecution of child sexual abuse cases in a home-like facility with professionals trained in child investigation. She has recently retired after twenty years as director of the Tanner Lectures on Human Values at the University of Utah, which sponsors presentations on ethics by noted philosophers and scientists.

J. Frederick ("Toby") Pingree holds an MBA from Harvard Business School, where he graduated with distinction, and is the CFO of Compliance Information Systems, a computer software company that facilitates industrial and sports drug testing. He was previously (1974-2001) with the accounting firm of Billeter, Halversen, and Pingree. A fifth-generation Mormon, he served a mission to Guatemala and was later (1982-1985) president of the Quito, Ecuador, Mission. He is a board member with the Guatemalan Foundation, which sponsors schools, farms, and health services in that country, and with the Sunstone Foundation, which publishes *Sunstone* magazine and sponsors theological symposia. He says he started thinking about "why I stay" in 2002 when a Church leader suggested that those who have questions should leave, a concept he disagrees with.

Gregory A. Prince received a Ph.D. in pathology from UCLA and worked for fifteen years at the National Institutes of Health and Johns Hopkins University. He is the co-founder of Virion Systems, a medical research company in Rockville, Maryland. He has published over 150 articles in the *Journal of Infectious Diseases* and other professional publications, along with two books on Mormon topics: *David O. McKay and the Rise of Modern Mormonism* (Mormon History Association Best Biography Award) and *Power from on*

High: The Development of Mormon Priesthood. He serves on the board of the Madison House Foundation, dedicated to issues surrounding autism, and the national advisory boards of six colleges and universities.

Robert A. Rees has taught at UCLA, UC Santa Cruz, and the University of Wisconsin, and currently teaches at the Graduate Theological Union in Berkeley. He was a Fulbright Professor of American Literature in Lithuania and has lectured at universities in China, Estonia, Latvia, and Russia; he and his wife served as humanitarian service representatives of the Church for over three years in the Baltic States Mission. A literary scholar, poet, and essayist, he has published both in his field and in Mormon studies, recently as co-editor with the late Eugene England of the seven-volume *Reader's Book of Mormon.* He is a founding member and vice president of the Liahona Children's Foundation, a humanitarian project providing nutrition and education to poor children in the developing world.

Thomas F. Rogers has taught Russian language and literature at Brigham Young University, Howard University, and the University of Utah and is the author of two books on Russian literary symbolism and the works of dissident writers in the Soviet era. In the area of Mormon studies, he is the author of *A Call to Russia: Glimpses of Missionary Life* and a contributor to *Literature and Belief, By Study and Also by Faith, On the Lord's Errand, The Gifts of Christmas,* and *The Need beyond Reason.* He has also served as editor of *Encyclia,* journal of the Utah Academy of Arts and Sciences. Cited by Eugene England as "undoubtedly the father of modern Mormon drama," he has received special critical acclaim for four of his some thirty plays: *Fire in the Bones, God's Fools, Huebener,* and *Reunion.* He is currently a Church Patriarch to the Europe East Area.

Karen Rosenbaum earned her B.A. at the University of Utah and her M.A. at Stanford, where she participated in Wallace Stegner's creative writing seminars. She taught writing and literature for thirty-four years at Ohlone College in Fremont, then retired to what she calls the one activity she loves more than teaching: not teaching. She is the recipient of Best Short Story Awards from the Association for Mormon Letters and the Dialogue Foundation; she is a contributor to *Bright Angels and Familiars: Contemporary Mormon Stories, Dispensation: Latter-day Fiction, Greening Wheat: Fifteen Mormon Short Stories, Mormon Women Speak: A Collection of Essays,* and *Proving Contraries: A Collection of Writings in Honor of Eugene England.* She lives in northern California with her personal editor, birding and travel companion, and best friend, husband Ben McClinton.

William D. Russell is an Emeritus Professor of American History and Government at Graceland University in Iowa, where he was also chair of the Division of Social Sciences. He is a past president of the John Whitmer Historical Association, past president of the Mormon History Association, and founding editor of *Courage: A Journal of History, Thought, and Action.* He is the author of *Homosexual Saints: The Community of Christ Experience, Treasure in Earthen Vessels: An Introduction to the New Testament,* and *The Word Became Flesh: Sermons on New Testament Texts.* He is a contributor to *Differing Visions: Dissenters in Mormon History; Know Your Religions: A Comparative Look at Mormonism and the Community of Christ; The William E. McLellin Papers, 1854-1880;* and *The Word of God: Essays on Mormon Scripture.*

Cherry Bushman Silver received a Ph.D. in English from Harvard, with a specialty in American literature. While serving on the general board of the LDS Relief Society, she co-authored *Knit Together in Love: A Focus for LDS Women in* *the 1990s*. Later she taught literature at Brigham Young University. With the Joseph Fielding Smith Institute for Latter-day Saint History, she contributed to women's history projects, including co-editing *New Scholarship on Latter-day Saint Women in the Twentieth Century*. She is currently annotating the 1874-1920 diaries of editor and general Relief Society President Emmeline B. Wells and helps direct the Mormon Women's History Initiative Team, which promotes research and writing on Mormon Women.

Morris A. Thurston is an attorney, family history writer, and historical researcher and lecturer. After graduating from Harvard Law School, he practiced law for thirty-five years with the global firm of Latham & Watkins, specializing in trademark and copyright litigation. Now retired, he writes and lectures about Joseph Smith's legal history, legal issues pertaining to same-sex marriage, and life story writing. He is the co-author of *Breathe Life into Your Life Story: How to Write a Story People Will Want to Read* and recipient of a Best Article Award from the Mormon History Association for his article titled "The Boggs Shooting and Attempted Extradition: Joseph Smith's Most Famous Case." He has been a member of the Joseph Smith Papers Project and an Adjunct Assistant Professor at the BYU Law School. He serves on the board of the Dialogue Foundation.

more from Signature Books …

Jack Harrell

A Sense of Order
and Other Stories

"Jack Harrell's fiction is the finest we've seen by a Mormon author. He is a convert rather than a hot house Mormon, which explains how he can so strikingly conjure both 'the darkest abyss' and 'the utmost heavens.' Writing about redneck cowboys or more urbane souls, his creations are believable. He reminds us of Gogol, and as the noted critic Belinsky once replied when someone compared a young Dostoevsky to Gogol: 'Gogols don't just grow like mushrooms.' Nor do Harrells. His evocation of menace seems to me to recall the haunting mood of Cormac McCarthy as well—a no small achievement. Harrell's prose is impressive, his imagery captivating, and his plot-turns unexpected. He is unrivaled among LDS authors." —Thomas F. Rogers, author of *Huebener and Other Plays*

236 pages, hardback
ISBN 978-1-56085-209-4

"What an amazing collection—a knockout achievement that leaves the reader reeling." —Angela Hallstrom, author of *Bound on Earth*

Signature Books

Stephen C. Taysom, ed.

Dimensions of Faith
A Mormon Studies Reader

This anthology examines Mormonism from a variety of contexts including ritual studies, sexuality, folklore, comparative religion, architecture, collective memory, film studies, literary parallels, and Jewish studies. In fact, the essays deal with the entire chronological span of Mormonism from its origins to today: from appearances of Cain/Bigfoot to Wilford Woodruff's vision of the Founding Fathers; from Joseph Smith's founding experiences to Edward Tullidge's reservations about those events; from W. W. Phelps as ghostwriter to David O. McKay's natural eloquence; from Mormon women's fiction to Mormon writing on the Holocaust; from anti-Mormon films to healing rituals; from constructions of collective memory to the uses of sacred space in fundamentalist groups. This anthology will provide readers with an example of the entire depth and breadth of Mormon studies today.

458 pages, paperback
ISBN 978-1-56085-212-4

Signature Books

William Thomas Allison and
Susan J. Matt, eds.

Dreams, Myths, and Reality
Utah and the American West

"This book explores a wide assortment of topics. For instance, we learn that Joseph Smith's son David Hyrum never knew his father. His mother, Emma, was pregnant with him when Joseph was killed by a mob in Carthage, Illinois. But that didn't stop the younger Smith from trying to continue his father's work, which for him meant reconverting the Mormons in Utah and denying that his father practiced polygamy. However, women came forth and chatted with David, saying 'Joseph did practice plural marriage and I was one of his wives.' David comes to Utah feeling he's got all the arrows in his quiver to deal with these Mormons and finds out there are some arrows being shot back at him in this doctrinal debate. He was not as aware as he may have wanted to be." —J. Michael Call, *Ogden Standard Examiner*

318 pages, paperback
ISBN 978-1-56085-174-5

"Whatever your interest in Utah and its past, I will make a promise: each reader will find presentations in this anthology that are worth the price of the book." —Melvin C. Johnson, author, *Polygamy on the Pedernales: Lyman Wight's Mormon Village in Antebellum Texas*

Signature Books

Robert A. Rees, ed.

"Proving Contraries"
A Collection of Writings in Honor of
Eugene England

Gene England was stricken with brain cancer and died in 2001 at the age of sixty-eight—but his impression on students of both Mormonism and literature was profound and deep. Among the institutions where he taught English, creative writing, literature, and religion were St. Olaf College in Northfield, Minnesota, the University of Utah's LDS Institute of Religion, Brigham Young University, and Utah Valley State College. He spent twenty-two years at BYU, and at UVSC he began the first Mormon Studies program in the nation.

This legacy makes the publication of *"Proving Contraries"* especially notable. It contains more than twenty poems, articles, and personal essays designed to celebrate England's life.

310 pages. hardback
ISBN 1-56085-190-2

"*Proving Contraries* should be read as something like an open portal to an important and rigorous intellectual past ... One might turn to Margaret Blair Young's contribution, 'Gene—Sorry I Missed You,' ... and hope that many more of the 'next generation' of Mormon scholars will someday say, 'Gene, we're sorry we missed you.'"
—George Handley, *BYU Studies*

Signature Books

Robert A. Rees and
Eugene England, eds.

The Reader's Book of Mormon
(a boxed set of seven little paperbacks)

"The format is intended to mirror the enormously popular *Pocket Canons* published by Canongate in the United Kingdom beginning in 1999, in which individual books of the Bible are paired with introductions by famous writers … In the case of *The Reader's Book of Mormon*, the individual volumes are marvelously designed. Each features a striking black-and-white photograph that responds in some way to the introductory essay. The entire set of seven volumes is enclosed within a handsome slipcase executed in black and gold. As much as anything inside, the appealing size of these small books, combined with the exquisite covers, makes them very inviting to potential readers. For instance, my young son, a somewhat reluctant reader, thought he could make it through these volumes one at a time and even take them to school." —Grant R. Hardy, *FARMS Review of Books*

1,048 total pages, paperbacks
ISBN 978-1-56085-175-2

Signature Books